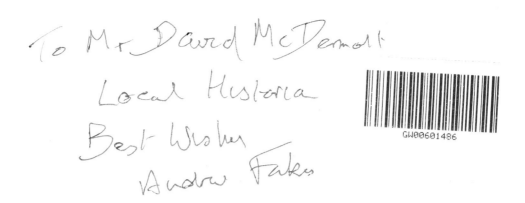

To Mr David McDermott
Local Historia
Best Wishes
Andrew Fakes

The Story of Hemsby on Sea

Based on the writings of the late George William Beech 1901 - 1979

Additional text, explanations and pictures by Andrew Fakes

Published by Dr. Paul Davies

67 North Denes Road

Great Yarmouth

2011

Printed by

RPD Printers, Gorleston, Norfolk

Front Cover - Top Picture: Hemsby from Ormesby Lane (Unknown Artist) c1800, Local Collection. This picture would have been painted approximately on the corner of Ormesby Road and Easterly Way.

Front Cover - Bottom Picture: George Beech sitting outside his house in the Spring of 1979 (A.J. Fakes)

Back Cover: Hemsby Church circa 1880, painted by Charles Harmony Harrison from the Moonshine Field (now St. Mary's Close). The man with the horses is Clifford Allen, related to the current butcher.

Note: Paintings are not exact copies of the actual view but I believe the thatched building beyond the field is the Barn Room and the church on the right is Ormesby St. Margaret (Local Collection)

Preface

Hemsby is in many ways an unremarkable village in that no famous or important people lived here. No decisive historical events happened within our boundaries. It was not until the early twentieth century when our magnificent beach came to the attention of outsiders visiting for holidays or coming to live permanently that many people knew of us.

This does not mean than our village and its people were not interesting or significant in their own way and we are very fortunate to have Mr. George Beech's book 'The Story of Hemsby on Sea' where he chronicles his memories of events during his lifetime. He wrote his history of Hemsby, printed and published the book by his own efforts. These books are now in short supply so Andrew Fakes has used George's original text and added pictures, photographs, and explanations together with a chapter on the way World War II affected Hemsby.

Andrew also notes some of the last of the 'real old Norfolk characters' who lived in Hemsby. Unfortunately, in modern times these folk have become few and far between, more's the pity. Over my nearly seventy years living in the parish it has been the home of many remarkable and interesting people who certainly made Hemsby a distinct village.

The book is mildly scurrilous and does not suggest that everybody living in Hemsby was a saint. Perhaps the most interesting tales are necessarily un-printable, at least for the present, but should you speak to anyone who has lived or visited here over the years, you could hear lots of fascinating stories regarding the doings, adventures and foibles of various Hemsby people.

Before Norfolk becomes as homogenous and bland as the rest of England I ask you to recall and celebrate the men and women of Hemsby who 'Done Different' and made it an interesting place.

Owen Church, Post Master for Hemsby and Committee Member of F.O.N.D. (Friends of the Norfolk Dialect). July 2011.

Writer's Note.

For several years I have intended to republish Mr. George Beech's 'History of Hemsby on Sea' in order to preserve his thoughts and to perhaps fund a permanent memorial to this notable 'son of Hemsby' as he does not have a gravestone to date.

My researches regarding Mr. Beech and into the history of Hemsby produced a great deal of information and pictures which, I hope will complement and explain parts of George's text. However, as I amass details of Hemsby, I realize that my writings are far from a comprehensive history of the village. So I place on record my findings in print as they now stand, otherwise I could delay forever. I hope others will be encouraged to research into the History of the Parish and where necessary correct my errors. A friend told me that when he wrote a book, he received enough information from his readers after its publication to write another book!

Please note that where I have added to Mr. Beech's original text, I indicate this by using a bolder text.

George's suffix to Hemsby as 'on Sea' is not the standard form of words. Whereas Caister and Winterton have the title of 'on Sea', this distinguishes them from other villages with the same name. However, Gorleston added the 'on Sea' to its railway station in order to promote its attraction as a holiday resort.

Considerable parts of the information I have used comes from the local press. This is now on microfilm and available at Great Yarmouth Central Library. It can prove difficult to read and it is easy to miss items which could be of interest but I will go on searching.

It should be remembered that East Norfolk was largely ignored by the Press and Broadcasting organizations until recent times. We did have the 'Eastern Daily Press' and the 'Yarmouth Mercury' but they had limited resources after the war. Reporters tended to travel by bicycle or public transport and press photographs were rare. For many years, the B.B.C. Home Service local radio news came from Birmingham. The B.B.C. began a Television News Service in Norwich on 5th October 1959. Anglia Television began broadcasting on 27th October also in 1959. We waited until 11th September 1980 for Radio Norfolk to begin broadcasting.

The earliest pictures used in this book were taken from post cards. Cameras for personal use were rare and did not always produce high quality photographs. Should people be taking photographs during World War II they would probably have been arrested as a spy.

I would like to thank the following for their help and information in the production of this book:-

Michael Allen, Alice Armes, Christopher Bird, Bernard Bould, Kenneth Chaney, Owen Church, Robert Collis, David Cook, Rodney Cook, the late Jack Durrant, Pauline Durrant, Philip Dyson, Helen Galloway, Nicholas Ginn, The late William Goffin, John Green M.B.E., the late Alan Hague, Owen Hanbury, Ronald Haylett, Brian Hewitt, Peter Jones, the late Florence King, the Rev. Anthony Long, Christopher Long, Audrey McDermott, Peter Matthews, Edward Playford, the Rev. Charles Powles, Michael Pickard, Barry Sharrock, James Shrimplin, Ronald Kinns, Geoffrey Smith, Pamela & Tony Smith, Russell Smith, Sheila Smith, Rex Steadman, Jack Stowers, Harold Tennant, Rosemary Thurston, Percy Trett, David Tubby, Christopher Unsworth, Joan Wacey, Patricia Wacey, Michael Woodhouse and Robert Wyer

Andrew Fakes Lawn Avenue Great Yarmouth

FOREWORD TO REPRINT OF GEORGE BEECH'S
A HISTORY OF HEMSBY [Published by The Flegg Press 1978]

It would be easy to say that the life of George William Beech of Hemsby (6.11.1901-2.10.1979) was a failure in that he died in relative poverty and some squalour but this would be to judge him in terms of material and financial success only.

He was born the second surviving son (he was one of twins) to Albert Adrian Beech a successful Master Builder of Pit Road Hemsby and his wife Jane (nee Cooper) on 6th November 1901.

He lived with his parents in the family home. They both died around 1960 and he did not marry.

By profession he was a woodcarver, sign writer and printer but without formal qualifications. His businesses seemed to do well up until the World War II.

Being blind in one eye he was not called for military service but I am left with the impression that his business did not thrive after that war.

The reason for George Beech having only one eye is uncertain. My grandmother, Ada Elizabeth Fakes, nee Larner (1881-1987) and the wife of his cousin told me that George was a very small child. His cradle was a shoe box. An infection developed in one eye causing its loss. The Rev. Charles Powles said that he got the impression from George that, during a clod fight between Winterton and Hemsby boys the young Beech was hit by a piece of clay with a flint in it which struck him in the eye. Mr. Jack Durrant his neighbour of many years also got this impression. I have also heard there was an accident with a pair of scissors.

The cause of the Beech family fortunes declining was, as George told me, that the Army took all the resources of A.A. Beech Builder and Brick Maker such as men, horses, coal and building materials for the war effort between 1914-1918. My Grandmother, who was not noted for being un-charitable in such matters, said that Albert Adrian (George's father), who was 'a handsome, athletic and talented man', got a taste for the high life and squandered his fortune and business away in London on drink and women. The Yarmouth Mercury records his bankruptcy in 1927. The rather splendid house he built called 'Homestalls' had to be mortgaged but it was occupied by the Beech family until 1979. It did not have electricity or mains water and drainage connected until after George's death.

Mrs. Ada Fakes and her great grandsons playing cards in 1980. Despite a ninety years age gap she could still win at rummy. (Nicholas Ginn)

There were several people in the village who felt that George Beech was a lazy and unclean man. He certainly carried out his work after the war at his own pace and could always find an excuse for inaction. I suspect lack of water and poor heating did not encourage the habits of personal hygiene expected today and he, of course, became less energetic as he grew older.

He was widely read as far as limited income would allow and from what he could find on the mobile library. His calligraphy and woodworking was of a very high standard.

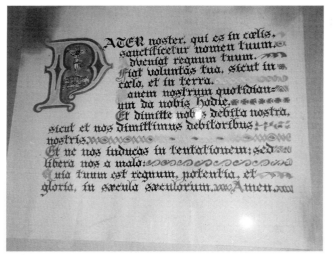

The Lord's Prayer or Pater Noster in Latin as written and illuminated by George Beech. It was 'drawn free hand' in 1939. George told the Reverend Anthony Long that he said it every night.

George Beech was a Norfolk Man and like Lord Nelson 'Gloried in being so'. He was also proud of his Norfolk accent which he felt was not always spoken correctly. He said that a true Norfolk man never dropped an H or sounded the S or the G on the end of words. His example was 'the horse runs away from something' becomes 'the hoss run away from suffon'. He was also in the habit of knowingly using the wrong word which sounded like the one he should have used.

He became unhappy that the unity of his village was being diluted and talked in jest of 'antelopers' from Martham but he says in the forward to his History: 'Yearly our true Norfolk population is diminishing ; although the general inhabitants are increasing , soon they will be the minority.' So in his History of Hemsby he chronicles the glories of his native village and its social and commercial life for posterity.

He was the source of scurrilous and 'off-colour' anecdotes, jokes and stories in an age when such matters were not available from the television radio or even in books. He took great pleasure in relating these to any suitable audience, usually in public houses, and the tale would usually end, 'Thank you very much I will have another half with you.'

There were many stories of a village character, referred to as Old Hitey. Anecdotes about him were long with notable punch lines. I recall the story of someone going into the barn to find Hitey hanging from a beam with a rope round his middle waving his arms and legs about. He was asked, "Whatever are you doing up there Hitey?"

The reply was "I'm hanging my ***** self!"

"You don't do it like that Hitey. You put the rope round your neck."

Hitey's reply was "I tried that but that hut (hurt)."

Hitey was supposed to have found a man a man in the churchyard crying so he said to him "Whatever's the matter with you?"

The reply came "I've just lost my dear wife."

Hitey, ever helpful, "Don't you worry about that my man. You can have mine until you find her."

Though not a devout drunkard he loved to visit the public houses for conversation, cards and darts. George's dart playing probably gives a clue to his character; he would wait to see if someone clearly fancied himself as a good darts player. He would then challenge him with immortal line 'Play you for half a pint, boy?' .The sight of an elderly gent with one eye, whose darts were smaller than standard may have encouraged many to take up his challenge. What they did not know was that George Beech was dart player of great ability and received many more half pints than he had to buy. I think it was George's great pleasure to surprise people who may have judged him to be a country bumpkin with limited abilities and learning.

One of his triumphs was the formation of the 'Flegg Comradeship of Artists, Craftsmen and Literary and Historic Students (Inaugurated 1960)'. This group consisted of several 'Young men about Fleggs (the villages to north of Yarmouth) who met for adventures, cultural exchange

Cartoons and sketches satirizing the adventures of Beech & Co by various artists. The drawings and comment are usually personal insults but without anyone getting violent. The picture on the right shows George (the taller of the two) and Morris Brooks going to slake their thirsts at the 'Bell'. Mr. Brooks was a wherry-man and you can't get much more Norfolk than that!

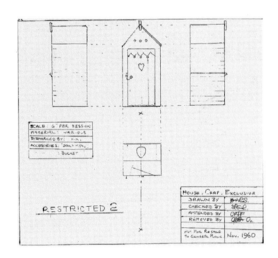

Irresponsible behaviour by now illustrious men. After a night in the pub, it was decided to put Mr. Durrant's privy on the Bell car park but this was frustrated by a passing constable. The building was hidden elsewhere. It was returned the next day.

An unflattering adaptation of an advertisement for SR Toothpaste shows that George was willing to be mocked by his friends. The cartoon of the modern Gulliver was drawn by George. He said that he was not an artist but he claimed to be draughtsman so the stupefaction of a large Irish weather forecaster being carried home caused him to put pen to paper.

The significance of these cartoons 'David meets Goliath in the Bell' with 'Little Webster' tripping up drinkers and 'The Straw Carters 1961' are lost on me except to say they represent some incidents of village life.

and carousing. They may not have achieved much which has lasted but they produced a record book containing drawings of their adventures and embarrassing incidents.

However, George Beech was living through changing times and his idyll of a full village social life was also changing to his regret, but young and foolish men get married and have to provide mortgages and keep their wives company instead of spending their time in public houses and in dubious adventures. Television, the private car and the breathalyzer also altered society in the final years of George's life

It is relevant to say that young women did not always appreciate George as he tended to touch people when talking to them. He put this tendency down to his being the survivor of twin children. Also his unconventional appearance frightened some children who thought he was a pirate because of his eye-patch.

I suspect that George had been thinking about writing a 'History of Hemsby' for many years and hoped to print and bind it himself as a magnificent volume but being a perfectionist he put it off only to find his printing machinery was no longer up to it.

I also suspect he was having thoughts regarding his mortality when he approached Bill Davies the Headmaster at Hemsby School. George had helped with the school magazine in the past and he asked that his book should be printed on the school's 'Gestetner' machine. Mrs. Judy Adkins, the School Secretary told me that George would deliver pieces of paper for her to type out as he completed them to cut the stencil. Mr. Davies advised her to type what George had written rather than question it.

The book was published as a foolscap edition from the Gestetner stencil stapled between soft cardboard covers in 1978.

Perhaps George should have submitted his 'Magnum Opus' to an editor or proof reader to make it clear what he meant in some of his sentences. He was keen to prove by the use of long and unusual words that he was a learned and well-read man. He also thought the use of the pronoun 'one' was the way 'proper' authors wrote. But, I am certain that his observations will be of interest to those who wish to know about village life in Hemsby over the years.

It is my great regret that I did not read George Beech's book thoroughly when I bought it in 1978 so I could have asked him the questions which have come to mind as I copy it out over thirty years after his death.

Although I question many of George Beech's conclusions, I would say that his thoughts on social, architectural and industrial topics are valuable particularly to the parish of Hemsby.

CHANGES IN HEMSBY

Hemsby had changed greatly in George's life time and more so since he died. There are many more houses and people in the village than in past times. The small army of farm workers who made up much of the population has declined to a few 'Agricultural Contractors'. 'Residential Care Homes' seem to be the growth industry in Hemsby in the early twenty-first century and they are the largest providers of year round employment. Early in 2009 it was announced that Pontin's Holiday Camp (formerly Maddieson's) would not be opening for the coming summer season and the site has been empty since but various developments including permanent housing have been suggested

There is a lot less unused or fallow land, fields have given way to housing estates and 'in-fill' development is the norm. Gardens are smaller. The roads have improved but there are many more vehicles and much of the village goes shopping in branches of national companies outside the village. It is generally tidier than it was with such features as neat lawns, flower gardens, drives etc. but cars and twenty first century rubbish are less attractive than rotting timber and derelict farm buildings.

Fewer people work within the village resulting in less socializing. The private car rather than buses and trains, allow people to travel to and from Hemsby without meeting others. Entertainment comes largely by way of the television. However, I note from the Hemsby Village Plan that there are almost 30 clubs and associations listed from Bingo to a Youth Club. Also, 'The Hemsby Harlequins' still manage to put on a Review and Pantomime every year

Hemsby is like much of England in general in that it has moved forward financially but something has been lost in terms of cohesion and community. I proffer his writings not to say that the period of George Beech's lifetime was a 'golden age' but in the hope his thoughts will interest those who live in or visit the village.

Many of the photographs and pictures included in this book were obtained by my mother and father some thirty years ago from people in Hemsby and beyond. I copied these onto photographic slides and the originals were returned to their owners. The slides were presented as 'shows' for fund raising for the new Hemsby Village Hall (Opened in 1985). I have reproduced some of these pictures and I hope I have attributed them correctly but if not please advise me. Also, I have not been able to verify some dates precisely. Many of the earliest pictures are from the Woolston Series. Mark Woolston was the owner of Hemsby Post Office at the turn of the twentieth century who published them as post cards.

As the oldest person in the Village, Mrs. Ada Fakes was invited to cut the first sod for the new Village Hall in 1984. The rest was of the work was carried out by Barry Miller and others. It was opened in 1985 and has been in use ever since

VARIOUS ANECDOTES RE G. W. BEECH BY HIS FRIENDS

JAMES ROBERT SHRIMPLIN, son of an Ormesby Carpenter, County, District and Parish Councilor, Countryman and one time Mayor of the Borough of Great Yarmouth.

"George was my friend and one of my drinking companions over many years. A notable Norfolk Man, certainly eccentric but good company.

When I visited George, he was usually making cocoa (this could be at any hour of the day). He would heat milk on an open fire stoking it with torn up pieces of cardboard. There were usually cats about the house all called 'Bink'. The one I remember was called 'Annie Bink' who was the matriarch. The cats were small and probably 'in-bred'.I remember one occasion when George and Mike Pickard walked to the 'Jolly Farmers' in Ormesby only to find one of the cats had followed them. The cat was put into a shopping bag and waited in the pub until her master's business was finished and then carried home."

"I once enquired why he was not working on one of his carpentry projects and was told in George's drawl, 'The light in't right, boy I'll do it when the snow is on the ground.' I visited him after it had snowed but George was not at the carpenter's bench. So I asked 'Now you've got snow, why aren't you at work? He said 'The snow's the wrong colour for woodwork. Tha's got a pinkish tinge to it boy.'"

"I feel George sometimes pretended to greater talents than he had. Bull **** baffles brains as we said in the R.A.F. and he was caught out on occasions. George often complained about suffering from the 'gut-ache' and he seemed to wear sandals in all weathers."

George feeling sorry for himself Easter 1961.

"I recall one Easter when the weather was miserable after a bad winter and George was pictured at his cocoa when a gleam of sun lit up his room. Beech drew a picture of the scene and gave it the title 'Misereri Mei'"

George's workshop spring 1978.

JACK ELIJAH DURRANT, Neighbour, Builder, Fisherman, Lorry Driver and Steam Enthusiast.

"Several of us boys used to go round to see George in the evening and he'd teach us the finer points of wood-work. I still have a mallet I made many years ago. We made wooden toys just after the war when little was available. The workshop acted as a 'Youth Club'. It was always lit by paraffin. He didn't like my 'Tilley Lamp' as being too bright and definitely disapproved of electric light.

There was always an empty chair in the workshop which had belonged to his long dead Grandfather On occasions the door would open 'on its own' and George would say 'Tha's Grandfather Emmerson coming in to see wa's going on' The door would be closed and later it would open again and George would say 'Grandfather's going again'. I never felt nervous of this. George got quite upset when a man from the Weather Station sat in the reserved chair."

Jack Durrant with Susie, his dog and Steam Engine. Regrettably Jack was killed in a motor accident when on his way to organize a steam rally 17th May 2006. Jack was very helpful in the production of this book.

For about fifty years Hemsby hosted a Meteorological Station on top of the hill on Ormesby Road and four 'Weather Balloons' were launched every day to monitor atmospheric conditions. As well as forecasting the site held a training school and many 'explorers' and 'television weather forecasters' stayed in the village adding to the social life of Hemsby. The station closed circa 2000 as weather forecasting passed to satellite technology!

Examples of George's intricate woodwork.
He would often recycle wood to make items from timbers salvaged from where he could find them. The rustic stool on the right was made from the old church belfry at Hemsby. Mr. Beech was 'green' and an avid recycler long before it became fashionable.

"I can usually tell if a piece of furniture was made by George. He always slotted, joined or dowelled woodwork where possible, He occasionally used brass screws but these were oiled so they could be easily removed. He always left dowel pins a bit proud so it would be possible to draw them out, at least this was the theory."

"I feel George's father did not always treat him well as he might and used to call him 'Silly Billy'. My Father and I gave George a hand to pull down the rotting wooden shop at the front of his house. George sometimes talked of a girl called Mary who he intended to marry and he worked on an intricately carved head board for the nuptial bed which was not used and I believe this was made into a settle and went to Winterton Church.

George was in the habit of feeding his cats with scrag ends of meat he obtained from the butcher. He used to chop this up with a cleaver and call out a cat's name for which one that particular piece was intended. One day a young cat got too enthusiastic and put its paw in the way of the axe and the bottom of its foot was severed. George rushed round to our house with heavily bleeding cat asking us what to do. My father said to pee on it which was done out in the yard and the bleeding stopped and I was told that this was caused by the acid in the urine The cat was bandaged up but being a cat it kept licking the wound and the bandage came off. George returned with the cat and asked what he should do so a finger was cut off an old pair of leather gloves and this was held by an improvised 'pair of braces'. The cat survived and the fur grew over the wound and it was hard to see that he was not a 'whole' cat. Most of George's cats were run over as Pit Road became more used by motor traffic."

"I heard that George lost his eye from an infection when he was a baby from Albert 'Sonny' Grapes (who worked for my father as a butcher). He went to school with George who had a glass eye at the time. He would take it out and tell the teacher it had fallen out. He would be sent home to have it put in but would not return.

The Beech family were in the habit of not going to bed at night during the war when there was a danger of an air raid but slept during the day

 Regarding George's mug, he used the same one for cocoa, soup etc. It had a tide mark round the rim. The shop keeper, Mabel dare not bend over near George otherwise she would have her bum slapped.

George was declining in September 1979 possibly through bone cancer and was so weak when they took him into Northgate Hospital he only lived a few days. Some people said it was the baths that killed him but he seemed to enjoy the attention he received in hospital."

M. Allen Collection

GEORGE BEECH'S FORWORD HIS HISTORY OF HEMSBY ON SEA

I dedicate this History of Hemsby to the countless families of Norfolk people who have lived here throughout the centuries.

The tall dour men who battled with the waves, many of them left their bones there.

The sun-bronzed farm workers who spent their lives on the land, which was watered by their sweat.

The craftsmen who left behind evidence of their skills.

The housewives of the past, who toiling in their cottages from daylight to dark without any labour-saving devices still managed to bring up families of ten or more on less than £1. weekly.

Yearly our true Norfolk population is diminishing; although the general inhabitants are increasing, soon Norfolk people will be in the minority; let us then remember those who have been before.

The Golden Sands, Hemsby

Hemsby. (Woolston's Series.) J 1878

THE ORIGINS OF HEMSBY.

Of the thousands of visitors who used our half mile of dunes and sands these last eighty years, how many knew, thought about or cared for that matter, how the village started. This is roughly what happened. .

About 1200 years ago Kendrick returned to Scandinavia from his reconnaissance of this part of the East Coast of Britain, after noting the sandbank between the Roman settlements of Garinonum (Burgh Castle) on the South and Caister on the North, which became the site of Yiermud or modern Yarmouth.

He approached the Danish leader Swegen Fork Beard and told him what a fine farming area this part of the world would make with rich pickings for his followers. Swegen (father of Knut who later became King of Angleland and had that dispute with the sea) agreed that a mission was called for. He filled his Orm Skibs or Serpents, their noted naval vessels and poured his troops ashore all along what is now the Norfolk coast. The few Romans, British and Saxons living hereabouts who opposed the Danes were quickly wiped out and the Danes advanced across a large area, burning, raping and killing everyone in sight. That is when Melhamstead (Peterborough) was razed to the ground. When all opposition ceased the Danes formed the Danelaw and various settlements were installed. The East and West Flegg (flat) Hundreds comprised 24 parishes, the largest Danish settlement of the time was under a headman. In this village his name undoubtedly was HEM; all places ending in 'by' being purely Danish and meaning a town. Fleggburgh would be the capital where the Moot or Thing (Parliament) was held.

There are still many Danish words in the Norfolk dialect and the strict retention of the aspirate [H] denotes Scandinavian origin. Norfolk is reckoned to be the only county which never drops an H; although, genuine Norfolk people never [sound] S or G on the end of words.

According to legend there was a great battle on the fields on the North West border of Hemsby and Somerton. The farm is still called 'Blo[o]dhills, but I have searched the Anglo-Saxon Chronicle and Norse Hiemskringla and could find no mention. So I assume it was a tribal battle between local Saxons (Winterton Martham and Somerton)

This feud was carried on up to the first half of this century [the twentieth]

The above contains several assertions which do not stand up to modern scholarship but as GWB had no access to later historical and archaeological research I feel he should not be un-duly criticized over this. The current consensus is that there were undoubted disputes between Danish raiders and settlers and the existing population of Norfolk but the concept of Vikings rushing up the beach and slaughtering or wasting everything is an exaggeration. It was, of course, profitable for Viking 'pirates' to plunder Monasteries, Abbeys and Churches which had amassed great wealth. This did not 'endear' them to the only people who were keeping a written record at the time; they were the Christian monks and priests. There are records of Vikings kidnapping people for sale into slavery but settlement and trading was probably less contentious, with newcomers occupying vacant or underused ground.

It is true that Swegen Fork-Beard's men burned Norwich and Thetford in 1004 but his justification of this was a 'pogrom' of Danes in 1002 (The St. Brice's Day Massacre) by Aethelred the Unready. The merits of East Norfolk were well known to the Danes for several generations before Swegen. The Eastern side of England was known as the Danelaw when King Alfred partitioned the country up between the Saxons and the Danes after he defeated Guthrum, the Danish King, at the battle Edington in 878. Athelstan, Alfred's grandson united England as one kingdom but this regime 'loosened' it's grip after his death in 939 and the country was not entirely governed from the centre.

GHOSTS

Every village has its ghosts but those of Hemsby seem very elusive, Hill House, The Vicarage, Red House, The Cottage and Sea View were said to be haunted; but I never found out what most of the apparitions were like. The sole exception is the one at the Vicarage, which is said to be a servant girl.

The surrounding villages, however, are full of ghosts. My grandmother used to talk of the Somerton Coach, which came through here to Yarmouth, the driver being headless. Another old woman used to frighten us by talking about 'Hyter Spirits' possibly from the Norse 'Hyter Gulrieg'

THE MANOR OF HEMSBY.

According to the Domesday Book in 1085 [1086] it was held by William Beaufoe and at his death, Herbert de Losinga, Bishop of Norwich, who, on the foundation of the Priory of Norwich settled it **[The income generated from the village]** on that convent. It was then granted in fee of £70.00 p.a. to Henry Marsh. In 1280 Roger De Hemsby granted a certain rent to William de Walsham the Prior.

'Hemsby Great Barn'. Although this barn has been greatly modified over the years, parts of it date to the 14th Century when the Prior of Norwich had it built. It is possibly the oldest secular building standing in Norfolk (Copied from postcard)

Upon the Dissolution of the Priory by Henry VIII in 1539 the Manor reverted to the Crown and in 1546 the Dean and Chapter surrendered all their possessions to Edward VI which had been confirmed to them by Henry VIII and during the same year Edward granted them in equal part back again with the exception, among others of the Manor of Hemsby, The Rectory and advowson of the Vicarage which passed by royal grant in 1552 to John Dudley Earl **[Duke]** of Northumberland in consideration of the site of a Monastery at Tinmouth **[Tynemouth]** in that County. He was attained **[and beheaded]** in the reign of Queen Mary but his son Sir Robert Dudley had grant of it shortly afterwards.

In 1569 Queen Elizabeth recited the grant made by her sister to Robert Dudley, now her faithful counselor and Earl of Leicester of this manor, 30 messuages [dwelling houses with outbuildings attached] 14 cottages, 1000 acres of arable land, 200 of meadow, 1000 of pasture, 80 of wood, 1000 of furze and heath and the Advowson of the Vicarage [the right to appoint the vicar.]

Lady Godsalve and John Walker by lease had manors here at that time. Sir Thomas Gresham purchased the Manor from the Earl in the same year and in 1571 settled this Manor with Rectory and Advowson of the Vicarage on himself for life, the reversion on Sir Nathanial Bacon Esq. of Grey's Inn, son of Sir Nathanial Bacon, Lord Keeper of the Great Seal and Ann his wife who was the illegitimate child of Sir Thomas Gresham. They had three daughters and co-heiresses. Ann married John Townsend of Raynham. Elizabeth, Sir Thomas Knyvet Junior of Ashwellthorpe and Winifrede, Sir Robert Gawdy of Claxton. This Lordship fell to the share of Elizabeth and her husband in 1605, she settled the Manor on Nathanial Knyvet, a younger son. It was afterwards in the Paston family. Edward Paston being Lord in 1742.

Other Lords were:-

Revd. Tilyard M.A.

Benjamin Copeman

Robert Copeman

1860	George Copeman Barker
1890	George Barker
1892	Julia Diana Haggard (later Lofthouse) Last owner of the Manor of Hemsby [?] {She was sister-in -law the author Sir Henry Rider-Haggard}

The information on the Manor comes from the Rev. Francis Bloomfield's monumental work 'Towards a Topographical History of the County of Norfolk' (published 1810). It is perhaps worth pointing out that not much of it was relevant to the population of Hemsby at the time. Up until the Dissolution of the Monasteries, people paid rents and taxes to the Prior of Norwich or his agents. After the Dissolution, they would be paying rents and taxes to the people mentioned. John and Robert Dudley were famous in the history of England, but it is doubtful if they, or many of the notable people mentioned ever came to Hemsby but they certainly enjoyed the income from it.

ARCHAEOLOGICAL FINDS

Finding of ancient artifacts hereabouts have been pretty rare. We have nothing to compare with those of Winterton, where in 1750 a man's leg bone (pronounced so by the College of Surgeons) weighing 57 ½ pounds was found. [I'm sure someone is wrong]

In 1901 a Mr. Woolston found a British Celt stone axe in perfect order and in my time at school it was in a show cabinet there.

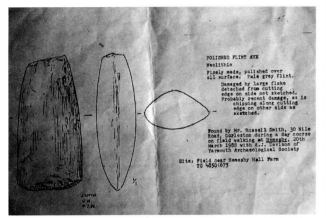

Left. A flint axe head found in Hemsby by Mr. Russell Smith of Great Yarmouth and District Archaeological Society in 1988. Recorded and drawn by John Wymer. A beaker type pot dating to about 2000 b.c.e. was found near Hemsby Gap.
Right. Roman coin found in Hemsby by Barry Sharrock of Somerton in 1989.. (B.Sharrock)

Jacob Hall found a Roman vase in the cliffs at Newport. Several hammered gold coins of Scottish origin were found when the cliffs subsided at different times. The last one shown to me struck me as a historic treasure because it bore the head of James VI who became James I of England on the death of Elizabeth in that year. I surmised that may have been lost from a French ship returning home after delivering to their allies the Scots.

What was reputed to be a Roman bath was unearthed on the site where Dr. Poole now lives **[Branton House]** on North Road, but the people who found it possibly were great grandfathers of our modern vandals. They knocked it into rubble which is all the experts found.

[Dr. Poole told me that he thought the object was originally a stone sarcophagus.]

Since the war when Mr. Guest ran the Guest House **[Now the Coach House Nursing Home]** on Yarmouth Road, he dug up some objects and notified the County Archaeologist who came over and examined them. They were said to be Anglo Saxon loom weights, surprisingly no further interest was shown in the site.

When one considers the Roman, British, Anglo-Saxon and Danish incursions along this coast and that the plough until fairly recently would dig about 4 inches deep it would appear there would be tons of artifacts under the surface. They should be searched for before the whole land is concreted in.

The 'Sanctuary Stones' in the village have caused controversy among the experts. The Rev. Gibson writing in 1801stated they were sanctuary stones but had the same trouble as I have had getting any documentary proof or even any official mention. In his time he discovered a base in The Street as **[it]** turns to Winterton Road. This is now in the churchyard near the War Memorial. A second was found in Pit Road opposite The Bell public house, this was found by Mrs. Pat Long and myself when they demolished three old cottages that stood in this site and removed it to inside the west gate of the Church. The third was supposed to be in the precincts of Hemsby Camp on Beach Road, I have never actually seen it. The fourth is now standing on the left (East

side) on Yarmouth Road near the Council Houses. **[almost opposite the petrol station]**
I dispute that these were (as some say) Anglo-Saxon processional crosses because the complete one has the same motifs carved on its post [base] as the font in Hemsby Church. This, however, is not its original location as it was moved in 1878, being in the way when the railway line was being put through

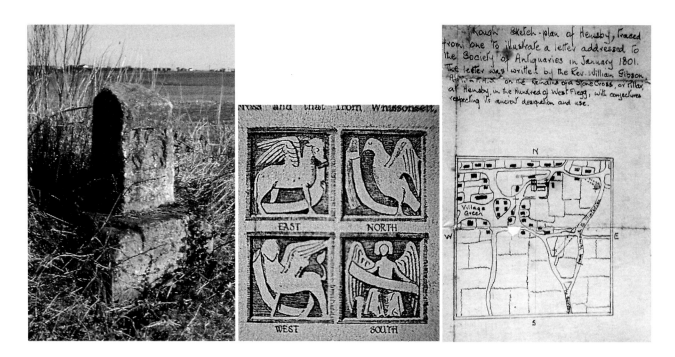

Left The base of the stone cross on Yarmouth Road said to date back to Saxon times but as George says the images of the four evangelists are very similar to those on the base of the font in Hemsby Church. (Photograph A.J Fakes).The 'Rough Sketch Plan' by Rev. Gibson shows a different road pattern in Hemsby. No doubt the railway changed much but Winterton Road appears to be further east than now. The Church clearly has not moved. I assume that the Village Green is the land in front of the Hollies.

A LOST HAMLET.

The hamlet of Sco between Martham and Hemsby was said by Bloomfield in the 18th century to have been depopulated for several hundred years so it can be assumed that it was a total victim of the Black Death in 1349.

A survey by Walter de Kirkley (Prior of Norwich) in 1275, Schofield is mentioned as adjoining Martham Field. Martham was subsidiary to Hemsby Manor at one time and the Hospital at Norwich and land therein [?]. Also mentioned was a King's Highway to Repps and a highway from Sco to Martham.

Our present archaeologists might find that it would pay to dig about there. It appears to have been situated from Dairybarn Farm to Rollesby Road, Martham. Perhaps the loke to the South of Gibbet Hill may have been the original highway.

NOTE ON ARCHAEOLOGICAL FINDS ETC.

The dearth of Archaeological finds in East and West Flegg left the impression that the area was largely uninhabited before history recorded people as living there. Indeed the widely respected archaeologist Mr. Charles Green wrote in letters to the Eastern Daily Press as late as August 1965 stating 'there was little settlement in Flegg before the Danish soldiers arrived in the year 897 A.D. as written in the Anglo Saxon Chronicle' Mr. Green had excavated at Burgh Castle and Caister and based his assertion on the fact that he had seen no evidence to suggest otherwise

The current consensus is exactly the opposite. The high quality of the agricultural land has ensured its constant use over the centuries since the clearing of forest began in Paleolithic times. The plough and the harrow have largely obliterated the landscape features (including burial mounds) and buildings left by earlier inhabitants. The lack of local stone suitable for building (excepting flint), ensured that wood was used which has rotted with time. Where stone was used it was too valuable a resource to be left and was re-cycled or robbed for new building. It has only been recently when such techniques as archaeological field walking, aerial photography and the investigation of 'post holes' has produced evidence of Neolithic, bronze, iron age and Roman occupation.

Also lack of early historical information is largely due to the fact that East Anglia was under Danish domination and most of the first chroniclers of England whose writings have survived, were Christian monks and priests who gave the pagan Danes a bad press when they chose to mention them at all.

Possibly Luke Ames' first boat purchased with gold from the beach
(K Chaney Collection)

The Scottish gold George mentions was probably part of a hoard of gold buried during the English Civil Wars 1642 - 51 at California north of Scratby. Mr. Kenneth Chaney told me that a relation of his, Luke Ames, found twenty gold coins on the beach after a cliff fall. He had a boat built with the proceeds. This was probably the first boat with an engine to be launched from beach in this area. Unfortunately, it is not certain what it was called. It could have been 'Grace Darling', 'Guide Me' or 'Elizabeth & Ann' Mr. Ames found 80 gold coins in his lifetime. Mr. Arthur Chaney (Kenny's father) recalled that on one occasion, Luke caught 18,000 herrings on one trip

The romantic idea of a lost hamlet is not what it may seem. It was probably a detached part of the Manor paying tax or rent to the mother parish and nothing more than an ordinary farm with the relevant buildings. The location of Sco or Sco'field is now thought to be where the parishes of Martham, Bastwick and Rollesby meet.

BUILDINGS

It can safely be said that from medieval times until the middle of the 18th Century the peasantry was largely housed in clay (lump) houses with thatched roofs and from then to the middle of the 19th century, pebble-tied with brick habitations were provided for them. With shipwreck timbers, sand and pebbles free from the beach these were built at a labour cost of £5. per cottage!

I can recall over 60 houses disappearing in my time -demolished with no trace, like the former occupants, enriching the land on which they had toiled with phosphates. Nothing is left for posterity - each little home simply disappearing with its atmosphere of love, sorrow, pain, worry and children's voices - as if they or their homes had never existed. Lives spent on the land worn out by the land and returned to the land, without a thought or thank you from anybody.

George was very fond of talking about 'earth closets', bucket toilets and night-soil. One of the most significant events in the history of Hemsby occurred in the mid 1960s was when Blofield & Flegg Rural District Council signed the contract with H.O. Andrews Ltd. a civil engineering company from Leeds to have the parish connected to main sewer. Much of the business of the Parish Council was taken up with discussion of night soil collection, cesspools and drainage prior to this.

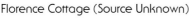

The house occupied by Mr. Robert Thurtle opposite the Congregational Chapel was originally two Alms Houses, sold to pay for the drain from Beach Road to the Post Office crossways (existing).

On the site of the Electrical [Television] Shop was a self-contained small house called 'Florence Cottage', formerly a draper's shop occupied by the Harbord family for many years.

The shop which is also the Post Office and is still in the Woolston family and possibly took this title when the Universal Post Office was instituted in 1840 (Existing)

Mark Woolston was the uncle of the mother of Owen Church, the current Post Master in Hemsby. Mark 'got by' with an untreated cleft palate all his life.

Florence Cottage (Source Unknown)

Left Hemsby Post Office Corner (Woolston Series Post Card circa 1904) Right. Hemsby Post Office Corner with Service 6 Bus from Yarmouth on solid tyres and horse and cart. [Post Card circa 1930]

The house owned by Mrs. Scott Drane now called 'Fantasia' on Martham Road used to be known as the 'Red House'

In 1793, when the tumbrels were rolling to the Place de Greve in Paris, the wild 'Canaille' clamouring for yet more innocent blood, and our 'Norfolk Renegade', Thomas Paine sat on the blood thirsty Convention, Dinah Manning, tranquil in her innocence of such things, one must assume, built the Georgian House called 'Red House'. She owned what is now Knight's Farm and her plaque is on the barn 'D.M. 1810' and the house 'D.M. 1793'.

Note I would have thought George would have felt more akin to Tom Paine as a difficult and 'bolshie' Norfolk man (from Thetford) noted as a profound thinker on democracy who 'done different'. He advocated electoral reform and felt that one man, one vote was the basis of good government. He is revered for his pamphlets and books particularly in America. Although he was involved with Robespierre in the French Revolution, he only just escaped the Guillotine himself. I think it was the writings of Charles Dickens' in 'A Tale of Two Cities' which are responsible for George's contempt for Paine and the original more benign aims of the French Revolution.

The Cottage Hemsby Street (source Postcard)

Another noted residence which still exists, is owned by P. Marsden Esq., late [**Headmaster**] of Great Yarmouth Grammar School, was for some 200 years the 'County Seat' of the Ferrier family. They provided a Lord Mayor for Yarmouth on many occasions, [**No George, Yarmouth is a town and has only a Mayor**] and the Solicitors of Ferrier and Ferrier, of South Quay, Great Yarmouth. The firm is now extinct but I believe the family still survives. Inside the precincts of the Cottage one could imagine one is in the early 19th century.

A Georgian House since demolished to make way for the Meadow Rise estate was called 'Hill House' and was built in 1815 for William Fabb.

Regrettably I can find no picture of this house demolished circa 1960

The cottages in School Loke are undoubtedly some of the oldest Hemsby abodes and have now been renovated in a very pleasing way. They originally belonged to the Pettingil family and then to the Allens. When Mr. C. Long was working on alterations and repairs a year

School Loke runs beside the school. .A.J. Fakes 1990.

or so ago, I found a genuine piece of oak mullion where a window had been bricked up - a genuine 16th Century mullion with a scratched moulding. Also the old thatch had been tied to the rafters by brambles; a very ancient method.

A hundred years ago School Loke was filled with thorns when the farmers cut their hedges for the use of the village 'bake office' run by one Ditchham Clark and the middle cottage had been this office. I noticed the opening where the thorns had been pushed in for the fire, the shelves on either side of the massive chimney hole where the pastry was accommodated until the customers called. Many people took their tarts, patties, pies and puddings to the bake office on the Friday. Thus as they were away on Saturdays in Yarmouth Market and couldn't bake that day, the provender was ready for them for Sundays. The charge was from a halfpenny to two pence per container. The bake oven was the same as we may see in Caister Castle.

There was brick floor about 2 ½ feet from the ground and a flue ran into the chimney opening. It was filled with thorns, burned until the bricks were white hot, when all the burnt material was brushed out and in went the tins of food and cakes. How they gauged the time of cooking is unknown, because once the goodies were put in and the one great iron door fastened no more fuel was used.

The red brick shop and house in The Street adjoining the 'Norseman' **[Public House, since reverted to its previous name of 'The Bell']** was built by George Wyer, Blacksmith, in 1909. He used the old forge at the rear which superseded a clay house in which Edmund

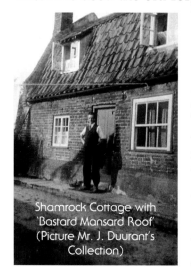
Shamrock Cottage with 'Bastard Mansard Roof' (Picture Mr. J. Duurant's Collection)

Don Pettingill the former smith lived. Mrs. Wyer ran the general shop. The forge is now gone.

Mr. G Durrant lives in the cottage next to the School yard called 'Shamrock Cottage'. This would be 300 years old, and it had a 'Bastard Mansard Roof' (after Monsieur Mansard, Architect of the Palace of Versailles). This kind of roof is pretty rare; in some old houses the spars ran to the floor of the bedrooms and one could only stand upright in the middle of the room. To obviate this, the Mansard roof (which in its pure aspect is a 'Queen Post' truss super-imposed by a 'King Post' truss) was used. According to the brickwork I should say it had originally been a barn, the bricks are Old English 2 inch.

The next cottage recently modernized by Mr. Jack Durrant has been altered throughout the years three times according to the brickwork. So it is possible the original was 17th Century. For the last 100 years it has been a shop owned by Elijah Knights and run by his daughter' Ruth Greenside, ancestors of Mr. Durrant. In the 1870s, Benjamin Starling used it as an emporium where he built harmoniums and furniture. Then F. G. Durrant hired it as general shop; His daughter Mrs. J. Salter kept it until 1930. Mrs. Greensides ran the shop until the last war and then lived, and died, there.

Next, up Pit Road, we come to 'Homestalls' occupied by the Beech family for 162 years. All the fore-mentioned buildings now come under the conservation order which embraces all Pit Road.

George Emerson set up as a wheelwright in 1816. He found a barn on the site which was used as a market garden only. He took lodgings nearby and transformed the barn into a cottage of five rooms. It had clay walls and a thatched roof with long annex at the back for the scullery, three coppers and a mixing room and a pantry. The cottage was destroyed by fire in 1916.

When Mary Emerson married in 1845 her father built them the wooden cottage one can still see. On his demise she lived in the larger cottage until 1911

[Dismantled circa 1990]

Left: Mary Emerson's wooden cottage. It has been suggested to me that its design is based on a 'Net Beating Chamber'. (A.J. Fakes 1978.)

Her youngest son, Albert Beech, built what is now 'Homestalls' (the ancient name) in 1899 as a carpenters shop, stables, hay house and office. He eventually built a further storey and the family lived upstairs. Later the shop was made into a dining room, pantry, and the stable etc. into other rooms.

Above: Homestalls in 1980 just after George died. It has now been 'gentrified' with such abominations as electric light, running water and inside toilets. Close inspection shows that corner of the house is not a right angle. A. J. Fakes 1980

The Pit a pond which was part of the parish drainage system.

Pit Road and Manse circa 1978 (Picture A.J. Fakes)

The ancient name of this road was always 'Church Way' but when the Emerson's saw pits were installed it was generally called 'Pit Road'. He had trees lying in the Holl from North Road to the Bell Inn, ready to be drawn to the saw pits. George Emerson did wheel-wrighting, carpentry and made furniture and coffins. In his time coffins were not planed but covered with black baize and studded with large brass nails to form panels. The initials of the dead were in lead foil letters about 2 ½ inches high on the lid. Silver for children, and gold for adults. Coffins were mostly elm or oak.

The Vicarage was built in 1845 on the site of the former one; it is now a restaurant because it was considered too large and unmanageable and a smaller house was built nearby for the Vicar.

[This has been sold and Hemsby Church is served by the Vicar from Winterton]

The Vineries on Winterton Road was a farmhouse with adjoining land and is not less than 200 years old, until recently it was in the possession of J.U. King. It belonged to several farmers, Byatt, Beales and Edmunds. The latter committed suicide in an out building earlier this century. Colonel J. Thorpe, lived there before J.U. King **[John Uriah.]**

The Vineries. For many years was the home of John Uriah King and family who were forced to move from their Horsey farm after the 1938 sea flooding there. It was previously the residence of Lt. Col. John Thorpe D.S.O. O.B.E. I believe he was a veteran of the Indian Army. Behind this farmhouse was a forge and blacksmith's shop. (Photograph J.U. King Unknown Date). Mrs. Florence (Florrie) King told me she took in evacuees during the War and 'Paying Guests' afterwards. She said that Sir John and Lady Hunt stayed with her shortly after he led the successful expedition to climb Mount Everest in 1953.

The Lodge in Hall Road was the Dower House to Hemsby Hall. George Copeman the heir apparent lived there at one time. It was a good example of a Georgian House and Grounds. It has been through several hands since the estate was sold and is now occupied by Mr. Ian Bruce the Solicitor.

'Chimneys', next to the Lodge was formerly a wheelwright's shop to the estate, the wheelwright being Robert Pestell (circa 1890). It was eventually altered into three cottages for gamekeepers and gardeners, and when sold was turned into one house by Captain Winbury who bought in 1948.

The Hollies now the home of E. Daniels [Ernest or Shucky,] was originally the Manor House and the cottage in The Street now occupied by Mrs. Minister was made from two manor cottages. Part of the Hollies is very ancient, but the front, I would say, in the late 18th Century, probably by the Revd. Tillyard, who owned the Manor, and the Living in the mid 18th century.

The Hollies or Home Farm. I recall Mrs. Helen Daniels allowing it to be used in a scene in 'The Dick Emery Show' and the fee was given to the Royal National Lifeboat Institution.

'Cats Row' [Chapel Terrace] on Yarmouth Road was built to replace an open yard of old buildings about 1890 by William Clowes Esq., who also built 'Hill Garden House' which became a nursing home in Kings Loke, near the beach. It was built where there had been a pond so continuously became water-logged when rain penetrated the rubble which filled the pond [?]

Cat's Row, or Chapel Terrace on Yarmouth Road circa 1904. The cottages have not changed greatly in appearance but note the lack of building all round except for Mr. Harbord's workshop in front. Woolston Series 1904.

Hill Garden House was the pioneer Nursing Home in Hemsby and it is now in a ruinous state. It was run by Mr. and Mrs. W. E. Danvers for many years. It also served as a 'Maternity Unit' with 'Nurse' Rouse as 'live in midwife' for many years. Patricia Wacey who worked there until 1950 told me she did not recall the cellar, which acted as an air raid shelter during the war, as being wet. Left. The picture just about shows the house about 1900. The trees indicate the strength the prevailing wind on King's Loke.

The Bank in the High Street **[now a Pizza shop]** was a cottage built about 1840 by people named Tooke. In 1914 George **[Musie]** Olley, a farmer and milkman opened a shop there. It was administered by his daughter Mrs. Grace Larter, and late sold to Mr. Denis Claxton who built a modern shop on the site

Station Stores in The Street .next to the Church run by Grace Larter (Picture Mr. C. Long's Collection). Mr. Denis Claxton was a bomber pilot during the Second World War and fortunately both he and his brother survived their full quota of missions. He is reputed to have dropped messages on Hemsby or Ormesby telling his mother he was safe. After shop keeping Denis went into the equally dangerous trades of driving instruction and later conducting driving tests. (Source unknown)

The dozen or so old cottages on the North side of North Road were built by the Harbord family circa 1840, and one of the properties was a sawpit and yard of John Harbord, carpenter and joiner. Most of these were damaged by a parachute mine in the last war and were demolished as was the smithy in Taylor's Loke.

A small cottage next to 'Lingwood' was built by Henry Harbord, bricklayer and chimney sweep. There were stables and workshops under the roof but the cottage itself only comprised four rooms. A feature of this house was that in the gable were diamonds made of wine bottles laid flat with their bottoms forming the diamonds. The motif I mention was very appropriate because this particular sweep was often found 'canned' in the holls that ran along Winterton Road. It is understandable because he swept the flues of the 'Great' houses in the district and of course in the cellars of these houses of these houses, were numerous strong beverages for a sweep whose throat was dried up by soot! He over-stepped the mark of Victorian morality, when he was found in a great house after sweeping there, in bed with the cook both of whom were pretty black.

Next to this hereditament **[building]** stood the long well known shop of 'Lingwood's' which was a longish cottage which had a glazed with slate roof butting out from its front to the road. All three sides were glass. This shop dated from say, 1850, and was kept by a little old lady called Angelina Lingwood who died during World War II. Seeing that my father can remember going there for his mother when he was in 'frocks' **[young children's clothing]** that would have been about 1873, so this old lady must have been well over 100 when she died. **[The church burial records her age as 94 on 22/4/1940]** Every conceivable thing was sold at Lingwood's. Treacle from the barrel, paraffin, household utensils, sweets, newspapers, groceries and in the shop window were flower pots , glassware and gaily ornamented chamber pots hung on their hooks for all the world to see. This building was damaged by bombs and the whole site was cleared to take a bungalow built by Mr. J Brown.

With a population of some 800 before the last war, there were about 12 shops in the village. Now with treble the population we have to be content with five.

If you could see the situation now, George, I feel you would have disapproved modern retailing in the hands of a few enormous companies.

The Allen family had three butcher's shops, one in Yarmouth Road, Pork Butcher, Albert Allen and later Leonard Allen. In North Road a Pork Butcher Jack Allen, and in Pit Road Clifford Allen later Harry Allen and presently Michael Allen and Son **[Geoffrey Allen is still trading on these premises.]** They originate from George Allen also a butcher.

Left: Michael Allen and Anthony (Tony) Smith
If you wanted to know what was going on in Hemsby the Butcher's Shop was probably the best place to find out! Picture A.J. Fakes Circa 1976.

Right: shop by Church kept by many years by Mabel Symonds and later by Robin Sizeland.

ANCIENT HOUSES (Continued)

The opening in Hemsby Street known as 'Picketty' Knights Opening comprised some ten cottages, a clay cottage with carpenters shop on the end occupied by Fred Harbord. This cottage had only one room up and one down and was always engulfed with steam because his wife ran a laundry. The area is now called Lexington Close, a tribute no doubt to the last owner Miss Alexis Dove. Why couldn't it be called Alexis Close, instead of some place in America?

Miss Dove was known as Lexie, worked hard and amassed property and cash but did not seem to enjoy spending it. I recall her gathering baskets of blackberries, which she took to Yarmouth Market and sold.

Hemsby Street 1950 (Post Card) The tiled building with notice attached was the fish and chip shop with many previous uses

Hemsby Street 2000

The Street Circa 1900 (E Playford)

There was a general shop originally opened a Pork Shop by Elizah Knights in the early 1880s, then run by Alphaeus Starling. Later it became a general shop kept by Mrs. Thirza Nichols and lastly by Mrs. Ethel Moll.

A former chip shop was built by A. A. Beech for Chas. Mumford of Yarmouth as a display front for his plumbers business. Then it became a motor repair shop, a general shop and lastly a fish and chip shop under various tenants.

Prior to the Great War some people named Burton built a wooden shop on the Beach Road corner **[North West]** (which is now Hanbury's) with bedrooms above, and later a dance hall adjoining so that village maidens and boys could learn dancing cheaply.

The Memorial Institute was built in 1920 having been originally the Y.M.C.A. building for troops in the Great War at Winterton. £1,000 was raised for its purchase and rebuilding and it was opened by Walter Scrimegour of Hemsby Hall. It had its troubles and had had repairs and addition. Where the car park now is was the bowling-green previous to the last war. **[This was dismantled in the 1980s and a new Village Hall was built on Water's Lane.]**

Hemsby Memorial Institute opened in 1920 on North Road. For many years it acted as the Social Centre of the Village for meetings, receptions, fetes, whist drives, meals, amateur dramatics, film shows and bingo. Though it was theoretically a dreadful fire hazard it survived for over sixty years until the mid 1980s. The barren land in the foreground of the right hand picture was a railway cutting about twenty feet deep in places. It was filled in so the site could be developed.. (Photographs A. J. Fakes about 1980.)

A quaint little cottage used to stand next to the manse on North Road occupied by Matthew Chaney, noted for his red herrings and bloaters. It was demolished in the war and a modern bungalow built for his daughter Mrs. Stella Dawkins. Previously an old woman called Hunt had lived there and she made duffel trousers and pants for men in the last century. The pants were flannel and tied at the bottoms. It would have been amusing to see her running her tape measure around gnarled fishermen and labourers.

Another small cottage, now gone, was in North Road on land adjoining the King's Head. It was owned by a recluse named Stephen Chaney (uncle to Matthew) who had exhibited bees to H.M. Edward VII. In his youth he sailed to Australia and had found some gold during the Gold Rush of 1859, but he was unlucky enough to have lost it gambling on the way home. Opposite the cottage was another on its own occupied by Harry Nichols and previously owned by Jonathan Gage, a Life Guardsman in the reign of Victoria.

The Guest House, 'The Gables' **[On Yarmouth Road]** was built in 1901 by A.A. Beech for Miss Bartlett who was an aristocratic lady. She did all ornamental trimmings for various pageants and carved the hand rails, door panels and mantle pieces for her new house while it was being built. This carving is in black walnut. A nursery and veranda was added by the King's doctor Lord Horder after Miss Bartlett moved. The House is now the Coach House Nursing Home

George is mentioned in a book by Mervyn Horder about his father Lord Horder called 'The Little Genius' (Gerald Duckworth 1966) but Mervyn mistakes George for his father Albert

Yarmouth Road Circa 1960. The brick building on the right indicates the Position of the Gables. Now the site of the Coach House Care Home It was a Guest House run by Roy and Lily Guest and accommodated many of the staff at the Weather Station. (Photograph T. R. Fakes.)

The house where Mr. Roll lives in Taylor's Loke alternated as a Curate's abode, a school and a laundry it was built 1811.

OLD TRADES:

Early in the 19th century times were hard with Napoleonic Wars flaring up and down and a large loaf of bread cost a shilling, a great drain on the labourer's wage which was about nine or ten shillings a week with no half day holiday. The smallholders and small farmers were as poor as their labourers and consequently wore themselves, their employees and their horses to death and then gained very little.

Carts used to call for children at 6 a.m. and take them to Caister 'droppin' a wheat'. A man preceded each child with two dibbers, making holes in a zigzag fashion and the children dropped kernels of wheat in each hole. There were fires at each end of the field for warming hands.

Frank Harbord in his workshop on Yarmouth Road circa 1930. (Photograph Harbord Family)

Through an unbroken line of carpenters the HARBORD family has wrought in wood here since the 18th century, from Griffin Harbord to the present brothers Alan and Jesse. Taking in, John, George and Frank. The old shop in Yarmouth Road has resounded to the saw, plane and chisel. Wheelwrights, carpenters and joiners, they also turned out an endless amount of coffins in their time. These were made out of elm oak and pitch pine also stained fir for those unfortunates who died in poverty or were washed ashore.

A. HODDS had a cycle repair shop opposite the church just after the First War. ROY NICHOLS a painter also had a shop in North Road, while his brother was general painter and decorator in Martham. JOSEPH NICHOLLS repaired shoes in The Street. He was also a phrenologist **[a doubtful science holding it was possible to relate intellect and character to the shape of the subject's skull]** and had a bust marked out in his shop. OLIVER COOPER was shoemaker in North Road for fifty years.

Launching a boat off the beach was not easy. It has to be dragged across the sand on rollers from well above the high tide mark and held in an upright position until it was in the water. For many years launching and landing was done manually until winches, tractors and four wheel drive vehicles became available.(K Chaney Picture)

The CHANEY family practically lived on the beach for generations. They are still represented by WALTER CHANEY [**Winkie**] fisherman and fishmonger.

Pictured are Walter (Winkie) and Arthur (China) Chaney with a young Peter Cushing whose keen interest in fishing may have led him into his later career as a Norwich veterinary surgeon. Right Arthur Chaney and Dick Warnes taking 'trips' in the 'Boy Pete' named after young Master Cushing. (K. Chaney Collection)

G.W. BEECH established a printing and sign writing business in Pit Road in 1918 which lasted until 1939 when war conditions stopped it.

ELIJAH THURTLE was a hay trusser and had a market garden. He used a large knife shaped like a skateboard which cut out the hay into trusses.

HENRY BLOWERS was a joiner and had a workshop in School Loke and later in Pit Road. He also ran a carpentry class for young chaps at the Congregational Chapel premises. It was said he loved to do intricate jobs in joinery and would spend days making special tools to do them and then became fed up. However, he did some good joinery including the screen and vestibules in Hemsby Church.

'TOOTY' HARBORD was a bricklayer and it is said that when he built the house near Yarmouth Road Railway Bridge (where Mr. Brian King now lives) [North of the Jet Garage]. He brought home a brick every day from work and then brought half bricks from the brick yard (3 for one whole one) [?] and his wife Kezia mixed the mortar.

RICHARD GOWEN [**pronounced 'Gown' in Hemsby**] was a carrier. He carried merchandise to Yarmouth for the public. Also at times he put three seat boards in his cart) and carried people in the manor of a bus. He brought back odds and ends for those of his customers who were unable to visit the town, His son, Richard Jnr. [**known as Little Dick**] carried on the business but he couldn't sit on the seat board because was of short stature , so he drove the horse from the floor, just behind the front board.

JAMES KING was our milkman and he used to shuffle round with his little milk float shouting 'Milko'. He had farm buildings which were recently removed to make way for the new road. [**At the junction of Kingsway and North Road.**]

Coal was delivered early in the century in carts by THOMAS LITTLEWOOD, E.G. KING and J. NICHOLLS at 1s [**one shilling**] a cwt [**5p. for 50 kg.**] Later ARTHUR TURNER delivered by motor lorry and Messrs Moy of Yarmouth had a coal shed and dump in the Station Yard.

MARINA NICHOLLS, lovingly known a 'Riney', lived in School Loke and was for 50 years Parish Midwife. She used to pay boys to get vipers from the sand hills and make them into ointment for treating some disease. People used many local herbal medicines and house leek was grown on many roofs.

There were no Doctors in Hemsby until the 1920s and doctors used to drive round in traps and gigs to visit their patients.

Until Mr. WALTER FULLER opened an orthodox Barbers shop and cut hair in a professional way, any one did it, some with a basin over the head.. Those amateur barbers were pretty rough. They snipped lumps off one's head at times and brushed one down with a 'dandy brush' usually used on horses.

Mr. Walter Fuller 'Demon' Barber of Hemsby pictured in his shop on the corner of North Road. This was a source of news, scandal and anecdotes about the citizens of Hemsby. He carried on his business for many years in spite of the fact he had one leg several inches shorter than the other. Walter was a 'barber' rather than a 'gent's hair stylist'. He would shave customers with a cut-throat razor as well as cutting, shampooing, and singeing his client's hair. I recall a minor dispute when George said "If Fuller can do his own sign writing, Beech can do his own haircutting." Mr. Fuller told the story of an embarrassing incident which happened because he sold his own grown vegetables as well as 'Barber's' products. An elderly and infirm gentleman came in and requested something. Walter was surprised but discretely produced a product from the 'top-shelf'. The old gent said "No you fool I said I wanted a fresh lettuce!".

ELONORA IVES opened the first 'Beauty Parlour' before the last war in Winterton Road. She, at one time, was hairdresser at the noted 'Shepeards Hotel' in Cairo.

Mrs. Ives Shop on Winterton Road (M Durrant)

HEMSBY MILL.

It may surprise the modern cosmopolitan inhabitants of Hemsby to learn that Hemsby had a mill at one time. This was a brick tower-built mill with several floors which was built by GEORGE DAVY STARLING circa 1845. He was a miller, farmer and wheelwright and his wife ran a shop on the site on Mill Road which connects Martham Road and Common Road. Mr. Gislam at present has the property.

Just before this century opened, Mr. F. G DURRANT ran the mill and as a baker and supplied several nearby villages. He installed a steam engine to turn the mill stones when there was no wind to turn the sails. He was awarded a gold medal in the All-England competition for bakers for excellence of his bread. When he retired in the 1920s the mill was allowed to deteriorate and was eventually taken down.

Hemsby Mill which stood at the Martham Road End of Mill Road for grinding corn to flour. This picture was loaned to me by Mrs. Patricia Wacey nee Fakes but it has been widely 'pirated' after I let someone see it.

[My grandmother Ada Fakes said that the mill was demolished by a man called Humphreys from Ormesby and that 'he had no business to take it down!' However, I was told that other people were pleased to see it go because it was unsafe and the un-controlled sails raced round dangerously in high winds.]

Under the manor there would have been a Manorial Mill in medieval times for grinding the community's corn but I have never located it. It was probably near the great barn or perhaps on mill hill.

A picture of Mr. Durrant delivering bread to Newport in his pony and trap.
In volume XXXVI part II (1975) of Norfolk Archaeology, Mr. George Rye catalogues the building as "a round tower-mill driving two pairs of stones, dwelling house, orchard, mill man's cottage. Steam auxiliary power after 1896. It appears to have stopped milling c1905, the erstwhile miller from now being described as a 'baker' which trade he pursued until 1920. It was demolished about 1924. The bakery survives as a piggery.
Miller's names Geo Starling, H. Warnes, Robt. Thompson, Walter Roper, F.G.Durrant

NEWPORT.

Newport is a fishing hamlet to the South East of Hemsby comprising about a dozen old houses with a former beer house.

It is said to have been formed by one THOMAS BOWERS circa 1830 and was mainly inhabited by beachcombers, fishermen and smugglers.

I have heard my father say that the row of houses gable end to the sea had communicating passages when he raised the roofs about 1895. Thus when a revenue man entered one house, the smugglers could run through the attics and drop to the beach outside..

Thomas Bowers was a canny fellow because his golden 'quids' never were secreted in a mattress or a bureau as with other people but were kept in the pockets of a 'morkin' or scarecrow out in his garden.

Some ninety years ago Dutchmen used to row into Newport to drink at the Cliff Inn no doubt bringing a few barrels of 'Hollands' [gin] for the landlord. The Cliff Inn was also used as a Post Office for Ships. Mail was sent to all parts in rowing boats from Yarmouth Roads.

Newport farmers were never surprised to hear their horses and carts rumbling out in the middle of the night. They would always be a keg of gin or rum in the barn the next day. Mum's the word!

EWPORT, HEMSBY.

The Cottage on the Cliff Public House ceased trading in 1914. Reputed to be the haunt of smugglers, it was a pub and post office combined and sailors would row ashore with their letters to post. The crew of the Cockle Lightship would also come ashore for a drink when not on duty. (Woolston's Postcard C1904). A 15 pounder gun was placed at Newport for Coastal Defence during the First World War.

[Newport was established in 1841 as a 'Beach Colony' by James Plummer of Winterton and others. They formed a 'Beach Company' hoping to profit from salvage of cargo and ships wrecked on the sandbanks. In January 1842 they had a large beach 'yawl' called the 'Royal Queen'. They launched their boat on 13th April of that year when they saw a foreign ship in distress. They reached it and left a pilot on board. They headed for the shore and within two hundred yards of the beach the boat turned over. Of the crew of 11, nine were drowned 'leaving six destitute widows and fifteen fatherless children'. A newspaper of the day wrote "All this occurred within the sight of their wives and friends and indeed within hearing as the shrieks of the perishing fishermen was heard at his own door." Newport did not recover as a 'Salvage' colony because most of the experienced men were drowned but several others seemed to have moved a mile south to the Salvage Company set up at California in 1851 (From 'The Beachmen' by David Higgins (Terence Dalton 1987)]

THE BRICKYARD

In the 18th and early 19th Century there were many brick clamps around here and several of the older houses were built with clamp bricks to bond the pebbles; but clamp bricks were inferior, being of many shades and they were generally out of true because a clamp, unlike a kiln, cannot be regulated in the burning. A clamp is a layer of bricks and a layer of small coal ad infinitum, and one had to rely on the gods to produce decent bricks.

Circa 1820, ROBERT COPEMAN, Lord of the Manor, having acquired more farms hereditaments, thought it would be advisable to produce his own bricks for repairs and additions to the estate. So, when a seam of brick earth (a special clay), was found on the Ormesby Road on part of Hall Farm, he built a kiln to hold 30,000 bricks. It was a rectangular kiln with two furnaces, a coal bunker, space to control the furnace doors and room for the brick maker to rest, sleep and control the burning which took place **[over]** three days and nights per kiln.

Copeman's bricks had round 'frogs' with a large C embossed in the frog. When the new Hemsby Hall was built in 1868 it was built with Hemsby Bricks,

Under GEORGE BARKER COPEMAN (Circa 1860 - 1890) the brickyard was hired by GEORGE W. BECK, and in 1895 by A.A. BEECH until the estate was sold in 1918. He had a lease until 1921, when the brickyard was incorporated into Hall Farm and bought by G. W. DANIELS of Scratby. Except for a few green bricks that survived the Great War no further bricks were made in Hemsby brick yard.

Little remains of the Brick Field to the west side of Ormesby Road. The kiln, equipment and even the hole from which the clay was removed have all disappeared Note the Weather Station on the horizon. (A.J. Fakes c 1990.)

Throughout the winter clay was cut down from the clamp edge (about 15 feet) by men with heavy spades called 'heaving tools'. It was then wheeled some eight yards in heavy barrows on 9 inch deals and trestles about four feet from the ground into a large heap near the brick makers shed where it was tossed and puddled by about eight men to make it fairly pliable. In the Spring the clay was fed into the 'Pig Mill', a square iron box about six feet high containing a vertical shaft with a series of blades. Attached to a pole about ten feet long was a horse who had the boring job of going round and round in a circle all day . The clay came out of an aperture at the base like butter and was planted on the brick makers benches at the back. They pulled it down with a curved crome which had two handles. It was taken up by the maker and jammed hard into the brick mould the base of which was bolted to the bench but the top was steel lined oak and could be taken off the base. The maker 'struck' off the surplus clay with a striker and with a deft twist he canted the mould and placed it on an oak pallet, a board 9 ½" by 5" by ½", and placed it on a barrow made of splines.

The new green bricks were stacked all along these boards on edge and covered by little portable roofs called 'hack covers'.

Inside the kiln, the bricks, after being sun dried for a considerable time were stacked inside the kiln, again on edge from the furnace bars below, to the top of the kiln.

There were four categories of brick- kiln bottoms, dark hards (or crimsons), light hards and salmons.

Members of the Dack family were conspicuous in the brickyard as there had been many generations of brick makers named Dack in Martham where they had two yards.

ROADS AND RAILWAYS

The parish of Hemsby is roughly one mile by one and a half miles it is approximately seven miles from Yarmouth and touches Gt. Ormesby, Little Ormesby, Scratby and Winterton [also Somerton]

In 1878 Hemsby was inundated by hundreds of wild, fighting navvies building the Stalham Light Railway which started from Yarmouth. This was eventually incorporated into the M & G N Railway with a direct run from Yarmouth to Birmingham. It was taken up in 1959 as part of the 'Beeching Plan.

No, George, this was before Dr Beeching's Report (The Reshaping British Railways) in 1963. The line originally called the Great Yarmouth & Stalham Light Railway was completed from Yarmouth to Hemsby and opened on 16th May 1878. Martham station was opened 15th July 1878. The line reached North Walsham on 13th June 1881 and was connected to Melton Constable and hence the national rail system 5th April 1883. The line became the Yarmouth and North Norfolk Railway in 1880 and was absorbed in to the Midland & Great Northern Joint Railway in 1893 It was losing money so it was taken over by London & North Eastern Railway (the L.N.E.R.) in 1936. It was nationalized in1948. It had rarely been profitable throughout its history so it was decided to close it. The line was in a very poor state after the war and would have required a great deal of money spent on it to keep it going. It was particularly weak at Caister where the sea was eroding the track. The last passenger train on the line was the 10.48 p.m. Yarmouth to Stalham run on 28th February 1959. (See Midland and Great Northern Joint Railway by A. J Wrottesley, David and Charles 1970/1981)

The road from the corner of St. Mary's Close to The Street [North Road] was made when the railway cutting was made. Previously one had to go from the eastern side of Meadow Rise to Beach Road Corner to get to The Street.

The Railway Cutting which ran beside North Road with brick steps and water pump. (Photograph by R. F. Bonny. G Kenworthty Collection.) The single storey building at the top of the picture remains there today. I'm told the embankment provided a great nesting place for birds. A further cutting remains between Hemsby and Ormesby to this day and I was told that a train was stuck there in a snowdrift in the severe winter of 1947.

When the North Road cutting was filled in it proved a marvelous opportunity to dispose of unwanted items which may prove a great source of riches for archaeologists in future because I am assured amongst much junk there are several old petrol pumps and an old Norwich tram dumped there.

An article in the Yarmouth Mercury dated March 1959 the reporter interviewed Mr. Albert Beech, (George's father) and Mrs. G. King who both saw the arrival and departure of the railway line in Hemsby, Albert Beech recalled 'playing among the boulders and soil from the cutting which was twenty feet at its deepest and was half a mile long and the only one of importance throughout the length of the line between Yarmouth and Stalham'. Mrs. King recalled as a girl of 12 she helped her mother cook meals for the gang cutting through their farm in 1876. In 1903, Mrs. King's childhood home (where the present Station House stands) was destroyed by fire caused by a spark from an engine setting the thatch alight. In 1923 they moved to her present house opposite the Railway Station and here again the railway played its trick for during the summer of 1953 a spark from an engine set the farm building adjoining the house and the stables.

Hemsby Railway Station. Though only a single track (non passing) station, it boasted a ticket hall and waiting room as well as Ladies and Gentleman's Toilets. I believe the first gentleman in the white suit was a Mr. Winter, a well to do businessman from Cambridge with a house in Hemsby. He had two sons described to me variously as 'idiots', 'retarded' or 'not quite the ticket'. They were called Foster and Guy and they helped out on local farms.

The station had a staff of four and the picture shows left to right Arthur Matthews, Bert Secker, Martin Diver, William Joice (from Caister) and Cyril Harrison. (Peter Matthews collection.)

Two photographs from sources unknown to me. The first is an aerial view of Hemsby Railway Station. The railway lines have been removed so I would date it at about 1961. The main B1159 road now called Kingsway goes from Winterton Road at the top left hand corner of the picture through the two buildings with white roofs to join the railway line as the 'Hemsby By-Pass'

The second photograph shows a busy Saturday morning on Hemsby Station with holiday makers returning home to London or the Midlands. I date this picture as post war.

The picture on the left shows the level crossing prior to the First World War. Beyond the cottage on the left the council office, bus shelter and public toilets now stand and behind the wall on the right is now where the shops are situated. Though clearly there is not a traffic problem at the time of the photograph, when the use of motor vehicles increased after World War II, trains stopped traffic on the main road which caused problems. (Source unknown)

The land from the Vineries to the Church and from the Barn Room to Pit Road was then call Stocks Close and was let for garden allotments.

Pit Road was originally called Church Way and led from North Road to the Bell and on to the Post Office crossroads.

Back Market Lane was the road from

The picture above shows the railway line being removed. (J.U. King Photograph)

Yarmouth to Winterton via King' Loke. The three 'RIGHTS OF WAY' verified by the Commissioners at the time of the Award in 1811 were:-

(a) The Gap to the Seashore

(b) Across Bridge Farm Martham Road to Somerton.

(c) From Yarmouth Road to Newport.

The path through Hall Road to Little Ormesby was only for workers on adjoining farms.

The Valley (in the Marrams) was also a right of way of course.

Until after the Great War our roads were surfaced by marl and broken stones from the beach, rolled down by carts of all kinds. One could see crouching on heaps of stones some poor old man, with a sack over his head and shoulders, breaking stones with a small round hammer on a long handle.

The payment for this work came from the un-employed from 'Poor Relief' rates

Sometimes visitors would give tips to these worn out labourers and one FRED CLARK was nearly assassinated by the rest when they found he had kept their share of the largesse.

Beach stones brought from the beach at the foot of Beach Road for road making. (Source Woolston Postcard)

40

Until the District and County Councils took over the maintenance of roads in this country in this century, the Vestry (or Parish Council) was responsible for rate collecting, road maintenance, the Poor Law and Law and Order. The officers were Parish Constable or Beadle, JAMES CUBITT, Overseer, JOSEPH EDMUMDS and Rate Collector GEORGE ALLEN.

Joe Edmunds, Parish Overseer. I assume this to be quite an old picture because the movement of the dog's head is blurred. Right Grove House was his residence on the corner of Waters Lane and Common Road.(G Playford)

The railway bridge over the Martham Road was demolished in 2006 (Photograph C1977 A.J. Fakes)

The Railway built two bridges; an iron bridge over Yarmouth Road and a Masonry Bridge on Martham Road. This was rebuilt in 1934 **[1926]** and is still there. **[demolished 2006.]** There were two wooden bridges over the line near 'Two Meadows' for use of Mr. Parry who lived at Hill House and kept bullocks there on the meadows. A man named Jack Suffling broke his leg when demolishing one of these bridges circa 1914.

Some cattle were driven to Smithfield **[Meat and livestock market in London]** by drovers -quite a long walk, but were later taken by train or lorry for slaughter.

Early in the last century the 'jeunesse doree' amused themselves by wrestling on the Glebe land on Sundays. They had iron toed boots to hack at each other's shins, probably a forerunner of Bovver Boots.

SPORT AND LEISURE

In 1885 Albert Allen, Albert Beech, Wesley Sutton and others started a cricket club under the auspices of the Rev. Harden who took much interest in the village youth. This was amalgamated with Ormesby at the turn of the century and became a noted club playing at Scratby Hall under Bert Nightingale. They would hold a pageant each year and have procession of bicycles, prams and carts all round the Flegg Villages.

A Choral Society was held in the Barn Room.

A poor tribute to the victorious football team ruined by the First World War but this is all we have to remember them by. The football pitch seems to be on the Yarmouth Road opposite Cat's Row. (Source Postcard)

Hemsby Football Club was started about 1908 and rose to great fame in the 1913-14 season. They played in two leagues and had the unprecedented record of winning all matches, home and away, during that season. As a result they sewed the badge 'Invicta' on their yellow and black shirts. Alas, most of the team were killed in the holocaust of the Great War.

A band was formed in about 1900 by possibly the most un-musical person in Norfolk, Richard Gowen Junior, who was clerk and grave digger to the Church. He wore a braided and peaked cap á la visiting German bands of the period. As far as I remember they could only play one tune, 'Our Hearts Have Met, But Not Our Hands'. This band improved, when, several years later young players of a more musical breed joined and it functioned until after the war.

Hemsby Village Band could it be 'Little Dick' Gowen playing the base drum? (P Wacey Collection)

42

Richard or Little Dick Gowen (pronounced in Hemsby as Gown) was treated by some in Hemsby as an object of ridicule and even contempt. Several people told me he was a quarrelsome man. He was a short man who acted as Parish Clerk and Grave Digger. He was reputed to have danced on the coffins of his enemies gloating over the fact that he had out-lived them. Michael Allen the Butcher said he believed Dick suffered from rickets as a child. Walter Fuller, the barber, recounted to me the story of Dick's marriage. It was said he advertised for a wife (possibly in the 'Church Times'). A lady from Wales was supposedly so impressed by his written overtures that she agreed to marry him before seeing him. She arrived at Hemsby Station and Little Dick asked 'Are you Miss ****** and she said that she was. To which Dick said 'You better come along a me then'. Walter was of the opinion that the good lady was not impressed by Mr. Gowen but pride prevented her from returning home as a single woman. However, the marriage lasted until death parted them. The Rev. Charles Powles told me that he remembers Dick as doing sterling work for the church in his various duties and particularly for keeping the church's heating system going.

I was told of two other 'ARRANGED MARRIAGES' in Hemsby.

An army officer got a village girl pregnant during the First World War. He felt unable to marry her so he arranged and paid for his batman to become her husband.

A man from a-well-to-do family was fined £10. And 15/- costs after pleading guilty to behaving indecently to young women on Hemsby beach (flashing) in 1922. He was possibly suffering from trauma from the First World War. The magistrates suggested his mental condition be enquired into. The family paid a lady previously employed as a maid to marry him and keep him on the straight and narrow. Both these marriages seem to have lasted until death parted them.

Ladies in Hemsby Church group circa 1950.
(Peter Matthews Collection)

The ladies had sewing classes and organized bazaars for various charities.

Every year a flower show was held by 'The Flegg Cottage Garden Society' in the grounds of a hall, changing the rendezvous each year. There would be a Bowls Tournament, a Military Band and large marquees showing flowers, fruit and vegetables in different classes for which prizes were awarded.

Village Sports Day was an annual happy occasion when hilarious fun was caused by the greasy pole, catching a pig and tug of war accompanied by large consumption of alcoholic drinks.

In the last century they held a regatta on the beach which included races to Yarmouth by yawls belonging to Winterton, Scratby and Hemsby but as the event became more bloodthirsty it was stopped. Pigs were put into the sea to race but they cut their own throats as they paddled [?].

Before 1914 the amusements were mostly concerts in Hemsby School when a stage was erected in the large room and curtains were run across. The dressing room for the artistes was the infant's room.

The football club staged many concerts and visitors performed for local charities. Some of the holiday makers were extremely versatile and gifted especially a party from Newport under Reverend Helder from Kent.

Billy Burton (a railway manager from Hull) introduced a 'Black & White Minstrel' group each summer. He played the banjo.

The Scrimegours from the hall gave a reproduction of Dickens' 'Mrs Jarley's Wax Works' on one occasion at the school with all their family taking part. They also gave kinematograph shows in the Vicarage grounds.

Darts didn't catch on at the Bell until 1939 when soldiers initiated the game in the pubs ultimately leading to the formation of three darts clubs.. One team started at the Bell in 1902 but a man having his nose pierced caused the landlord to ban the game.

In 1939 this village was well represented in sport, having four football clubs (School, Junior, 1st and 2nd Elevens), a Boxing Club, Billiard Club, a Band, four Bowling Clubs, Tennis Club, Domino Rings and cards were played in the pubs.

The car pictured belonged to the Daniels Family and is pre First World War and perhaps the first in Hemsby. (EX registration indicates a Yarmouth registered car) I believe the two girls standing beside the car are Miss Mary-Anne and Miss Lily Daniels. Mr. Thresher the Chauffeur told his friend Arthur Chaney that he got the car started by heating the plugs with a blow lamp. Right 'The Homestead on Beach Road with 'The Firs' further up the hill. As well as the car they owned a bowling green and when the Homestead Team won the Flegg League in 1933 George penned the following ode.

Hail Hemsby Homestead.

Victorious HOMESTEAD! In the Bowling World
You have secured your laurels: Victory's flag unfurled
above your name; for Captained by a PRATT ,
You've licked the Flegg League Die-hards and knocked them flat.
With technique of a BLOWERS, TYSON'S skill
allied with that of KNIGHTS you had the will
To play to win, and favoured by the Graces,
you won the Caister Cup; put rivals in their places.
For all of you fine players, united Youth and Age
Have striven on the green and left the page
of sport unsullied, clean and virgin white,
For, though you won your games, 'twas in fair fight
and now the seasons ended, brothers of the Green,
Your sideboard filled with Trophies and the sheen
Of all the Challenge Cups that you can muster
Make all the Hemsby Bowlers proud; reflect the lustre
of your fame.
Courageous Homestead through matches you have won galore,
That fighting spirit must remain in Nineteen Thirty Four

1933   Rusticus.

VILLAGE SOCIAL LIFE (Continued)

Victorian children played rounders, tops, cross cabbage and marbles. Edwardian children enjoyed tops, hoops, marbles and a game learned by volunteers in the Boer War called 'Ship a Bunna'. I have never seen this game played since 1914.

A favourite game of the older boys was to work across Hemsby Bridge hand over hand on a pipe holding the signal wire. It was about 15 feet above the road so it is miraculous that someone wasn't killed. There was always plenty of ammunition for fights, loads of stones being dumped near the school for road repairs and some Saturdays we filled our pockets and went to the Winterton boundary in the valley and had pitched battles with the Winterton boys.

Unlike the present age, Edwardian Hemsby tolerated no vandalism. Too many hands were against boys, but they had their fun when possible. One sport arose from the fact farm workers went to bed early, having to rise early and in summer left their windows oven. Boys used to get on one another's backs and throw clods at the people in bed! This was obviated, however, by men being prepared, and as the boy's head arose above the window sill, the occupants would empty the 'Jerry' over them.

Concerts given by children in the 1930s under Mr. E. A. England were extremely well performed and received.

Small fairs would occasionally visit Hemsby, notably those of Gray and 'Old Rhubarb' otherwise Underwood. They would contain the usual amusements.

At the beginning of the century Russians with dancing bears and 'Cheap-Jacks' selling crockery on the 'Bell' plain. One ancient individual used to bring a donkey drawn emporium in which snakes in bottles, fossils, skeletons and stuffed birds. This exhibition got a few coppers from the school children. Once some young sparks unyoked his donkey and pushed it [?] down the steps of the bar of the old Bell causing panic to those drinking there. He must have been pretty old because my father said his show came round when he was a boy.

The celebration of the Coronation of Edward VII (1902) was held in the field which Seacroft Camp now stands [**North of Beach Road.**] That of George V in 1911 took place on the 'Moonshine' [**now St. Mary's Close.**] We were given mugs bearing the royal portrait. The Jubilee of George V was at Maddieson's Camp with a huge bonfire and refreshments. That of George VI (1937) was at Seacroft Camp with refreshments and a bowling tournament.

In 1911, a full meal was served in Hemsby School but there was no beer! Several patriotic citizens, including my father objected to the committee consisting of radicals and teetotalers and said it was a tradition that all present should drink the King's health. The committee could drink water if they wished (chacun a son gout) but they intended to drink his health in beer and let the elders try to stop them!

Prior to the Enclosure Act passed by Parliament in 1810, the Village Green was off Waters Lane in front of the Manor House (The Hollies) and in medieval times there was an ordinance issued that all young men practice the 'long bow' on village greens on Sunday (the only holiday they had), instead of indulging in such ungodly games as football. Football at that time was not the precise game it now is. The whole village would take sides. There was no boundary and the ball was an enormous skin stuffed with rags. Several people were killed or crippled at each match.

The award gave this land to Mary Ferrier whose property adjoined. Today it is beautifully laid out and, in spring is very pleasing with hundreds of daffodils and weeping willows.

[**The**] 'Poor Land' consisted of ten acres left by a dower and 15 acres under the Enclosure Act consolidated under [**the**] Charity Commissioners in 1873. The rents [**received**] were used to buy coal which was distributed to the poor of the parish.

HEMSBY CHURCH

Hemsby Church, circa 1800. The chancel roof appears to be thatched but the nave is possibly slate. The roof line on the tower shows the original church roof was at a much steeper angle.

This picture contradicts some of the church guides which state that the nave and chancel are all of a piece. The artist is believed to be Thomas Ladbroke (Local Collection)

Our church, dedicated to St. Mary the Virgin, consists of Chancel, Nave and South Porch in the perpendicular style with a square embattled tower containing a clock erected (installed) 1870. Originally there were five bells in its belfry. The belfry was removed as unsafe in the 1920s, being eaten up with beetle and never rebuilt but one bell was left to strike the hours. Another was sold early in the century, being cracked, and the others rested in the Nave, awaiting endlessly to be restored to the belfry. They were hung in 1660, the year of the restoration of Charles II. For the record these grounded bells were stolen a few years ago [1972] but Rev. Briggs was lucky enough to trace them to Essex and get them returned.

The previous year one of the Hemsby Bells was donated to the Chapel of Trinity College, Kandy, Ceylon or Sri Lanka as we now call it.

Hemsby Church from the air circa 1990. The building on the right of the church, the Spar Shop was replaced by houses in 2006-7. The grassed area on the top right of the picture is Hemsby's new burial ground consecrated in June 1974. Later that year the Church Tower was re-pointed. (Copyright Norfolk Archaeological Unit.)

The church was restored in the heyday of Victorian religious fervour, in 1868 when all the new seating was installed. The oak pews were said to have been sawn from one oak tree grown at Rollesby and the joinery made up in the Barn Room. About 1906 Vestibules were built over each door to obviate draught [draft] and the screen was given a cornice with a tabernacle above. There is also a Rood loft with staircase. In 1950 when the roof was rebuilt, holes were found in the parvise above the porch where bunks had been erected some 500 years earlier. These were used by the Monks of St. Benet's Abbey when attached to this church for service. **[It could have equally been used by watchmen who guarded the church]** In 1920 the roof of the tower was replaced by Fakes and Blowers and re-laid with lead. The old lead (1721) was completely covered by tracings of feet with initials going back some 200 years and one could note the change in shape of the footwear.

There is a fine memorial tablet to the Rev. Robert Tilyard M.A. 1786 in Latin. He was Rector and Lord of the Manor at that time. There is also a fine stained glass window in the South East Wall to Rev. Henry Harden B.A.

Above the church porch is 'the Priest's Room' perhaps for visiting priests or church caretaker and guardian. It has been used as a classroom but it is not for the claustrophobic.

The Copeman family are interred in the chancel. The writer's grandparent built the brick graves for most of them and when digging for one my father found a small skull covered in golden hair, but when he held it up to show his father it disintegrated. A small gravestone had been lying about for many years and I eventually persuaded [the] authorities to have it moved and sheltered in the church because it bears an historic date - 1665 the Plague year! This stone was never in the churchyard. It had been bedded down and was no doubt the memorial of Margaret Thompson the skull of whom my parent unearthed.

The Ferrier family lie along the aisle and in three vaults in the yard. One can see where their brasses have been removed.

Richard (Dick) Bagnall-Oakley, son of the Vicar of Hemsby, (born 1908). He went on to become a respected teacher at Gresham's School near Holt. A noted naturalist and broadcaster. He was an advocate of the Norfolk dialect. He put this down to his attending Hemsby School for a time. He addressed his school friends in the refined accents of the Vicarage and was mocked by his classmates, so he adopted a Norfolk accent but when he used the local pronunciations at home he was castigated by his parents. He said that this situation forced him to be bi-lingual to keep out of trouble and, he was always grateful for that. He died in 1974 just after his retirement.

Regarding the Sanctuary Cross bases in the churchyard it may be well to explain that prior to the Reformation of Henry VIII, as churches were Roman Catholic the Pope's Law surmounted the King's Law. Consequently any felon sought by the Constable for an offence "when once he had reached the Alter, frid - stoll [?], chancel or any other sanctified part and put himself under its protection; his person became sacred and protected by its influence even if they departed from it a certain number of paces round the church". A refugee from justice would be allowed to remain in this sanctified area for fifteen days although allowed out to empty his bowels. After this period in which the law couldn't touch him, he had to surrender or 'adjure' the realm, in which case he was pardoned on condition he walked to a specified port holding a wand in his hand and reporting to the Constable (Beadle) in every village or township through which he passed. He was then put on a ship to wherever the captain wished having to adjure the realm for life,

I can imagine these poor wretches landing in slavery on the Barbary Coast unless the Masters of ships just dumped them in the channel. No one would have known of or cared.

This climate has eaten away the moulded stones of our church continuously and all except the tower which I assume to be Caen Stone, have been replaced in my lifetime,

Before the restoration of the roof [this] was partly thatch and partly lead. The gates bearing St. Mary's emblem were erected in 1936.

The organ was replaced by a modern console, was a large oak paneled affair installed in 1906 by A.A. Beech and H.B. Blowers. The organ was built in London and cost £1000. (quite a sum for those days) defrayed by W. Scrimegour Esq. It was worked by hand by means of a lever on a bellows , quite a soul destroying job

Hemsby Church Gates made by George William Beech in 1936.

I recall my father saying he was very pleased to pump the organ because got three pence per service for that job AJF.

There are several vaults in the churchyard and a special site was made for those poor friendless bodies which washed ashore and were buried by the parish. One more recent, was that of Janis Galli, a Latvian Seaman who was returning from the South Atlantic when his ship the 'Tautmila' was damaged by enemy action off Haisboro' and brought into Yarmouth. He was found dead in a small boat in 1940. Latvia was a neutral country then, so after repairs the ship returned home the man's father sent the Vicar a photo of his son, which was displayed in the Vestry.

A memorial Ionic Cross by Perfitt's of Stalham was erected in the churchyard in 1921 in memory of those who lost their lives in the Great War, and after the Second War, this was incorporated in a symbolic wall with the names of the dead [of WW II]

The Dedication of the War Memorial to the fallen of The First World War. [1920]. The original War Memorial had an iron fence but a recess was cut in the wall for the WW II memorial.

Hemsby War Memorials. Twenty young men were killed in the Great War and World War II claimed eight lives of servicemen.

Mr. Anthony Long has mounted a brass found in the yard, believed to be a patina from a coffin of an ecclesiastic it is mounted at the south wall of the church.

A market was granted in 1225 by the Prior of Norwich.

[Very nice of him but as he taxed the traders it was not just a favour to the citizens of Hemsby]

List of Incumbents:

1255 William Foteshun
1324 Robert de Langdale
1328 William de Bybham
1333 John Goodrych
1340 Roger Petroun.
1355 John de Steynaston
1394 Oliver Mendham
14-- Jeffrey Danyell
1448 Edmund Trynok
1498 John Tedney
15-- John Holt
1552 George Yockers
1600 John Green B.A.
16-- Thomas Lewgar
1624 Nathanial Tilney
1643 Robert Hooke

1667 Thomas Bradford
1682 Charles Coates
1728 Richard Marye
1728 Thomas Waites
1770 Robert Tiyard M.A. Also Patron
1787 Thomas Kerrick
1805 Robert Hales
1853 Clement Gilbert
1864 Henry William Harden B.A.
1896 Kemeys Leoline Pearce Church Bagnall-Oakley
1933 William Howard Wilson Pipe
1936 Basil George Dunmore Clark B.A.
1958 Harry FitzHerbert Briggs
1972 Christopher George Clarke
1978 Richard Page

In the 18th century there was a memorial with the inscription:-
Orate p.a.I. A Thomas Bunne qui pavement hujus ecclie
Lapidus memories fieri fecit A DNI 1500
Don't worry about the dog-Latin, reader, all it boils down to:-
Pray for the soul of Thomas Bunne, who did have the floor of this church paved with marble stones A.D 1500.

A Tablet to the Glasspoole family is on the South wall of the aisle,

(A) Memorial window with the arms of 'Baconne, Stanhoe, and Farleye and another with the arms of Dooke have all disappeared .These are mentioned in the Harleian Collection of M.S.S.

A tablet to Rev Oakley 1933, a brass to Capt. Mark Haggard.

A memorial tablet in the chancel to Richard Ferrier 1933, Madeline Lucy his wife and Robert their son 1917,

A stained glass window to Rev. H. Harden in the chancel. A small stained glass window with the arms of Ferrier.

A bronze plaque to those killed in the Great War.

[An] Oak screen in the vestry in memory of David Turner, killed as a child.

A reading desk to R.C. Jones Schoolmaster.

A small reading desk for Sunday School in memory of two war dead. George Loades and Cubitt Armes.

SCHOOLS

The earliest seat of bucolic learning seems to have been the 'Dame School' in the house now occupied by Mr. Roll in Taylor's Loke, while Lady of the Manor, Mrs. Robert Copeman, gave elementary teachings and 'Penny Readings' to people of all ages in Newport once a week.

The first orthodox school, built by the Manor and controlled by the Church was installed next to the Church in 1841. It had paid teachers and the pupils had to contribute a few pence a week. The labouring classes, having anything up to 12 children per family could only afford the education of perhaps two of their children until the Education Act of 1870 brought universal free education [for those up to the age of eleven]. The masters drove it into the pupils in a Victorian manner, with copious administration of the cane. The shop now known as 'Spar' [Beside the church, pulled down 2006] was originally the Schoolmaster's house but when the school burned down on February 16th 1900, the village got together to arrange for a new modern school and the Manor gave them enough land in Pit Road to build it and also a new Head Teacher's house. It was reckoned at the time to be a model elementary school for 200 scholars, and pleasingly designed by T. Inglis-Goldie who was also the architect for Caister Cemetery Chapel. The builder was A.A. Beech and the bricks (excluding the moulded bricks) were made in Hemsby.

Hemsby School just after it was built. None of the trees that now surround the buildings have grown. All the girls seem to be wearing white smocks. (Post Cards Possibly Woolston Series)

The double gabled house next to the old school, owned by Mrs. R. Long was built for the schoolmaster's house, the bungalow being too small for Mr. Brook's large family. This reverted to the Manor, who built it, when the new school house was used.

The village school was opened in 1902 and its first headmaster was Richard Cobden Jones [always called R.C by my father]. He retired in 1925 to his retreat 'Elmsfield' School Loke, so that he could always see and hear the children he loved.

His successor was Arthur England, since retired, a veteran of World War One.

A sad detail regarding Mr. England, He and his wife had one son, John, who was captured by the Germans in WW II but he escaped and returned to fight. He was a lieutenant in the Parachute Regiment when he was killed on 24th March 1945 aged 22. He is mentioned on the War Memorial as J England M.B.E.

Mr. (Edward) Arthur England, Headmaster of Hemsby School from 1926-1955, presenting Jean Dove with shield for athletics Mr. England was joined Kitchener's Army in 1914. He was injured in the thigh on the 1st July 1916. During the first day of the Battle of the Somme. He recovered and went back to fight only to be injured again in February 1917 when he almost lost both legs. On retirement Mr. England moved to Yarmouth and went on to live a full and active life playing golf and bowls. He died at the age of 103 years in 1993.

Hemsby School 1922 .Back Row left to right Bob Crowe, Arthur Utting, (Leonard) Jimmy Knights, Bert Fakes, Dick Brown, Stanley Lawson, Sidney Smith , Walter Fuller, Walter Powles. Middle row, Ivy Etheridge, Netty Spooner, Thelma Greensides, Blanche King, Rhoda Allen, Rosa Knights, Arthur Fakes, Jack Thurtle, (Sticky). [Jack became a blacksmith but was struck by rheumatic fever in his youth. Although he was able to go back to this trade he walked with a stick.] Front Row Jack King, Victor Boate, Arthur Chaney, Eve Loades, Rosie Knights, Doris Long, Louie Porter, May Thompson, Connie King. (Thanks to Geoffrey Smith and Kenny Chaney for their help with this picture)

Pit Road and School shortly after W.W.II from Church Tower. Note blast walls at front of School. The field where the horses are ploughing is now the housing development called Stable Field. (Photograph M. Allen)

CHAPELS

The earliest known chapel was the bungalow since modernized by P.C. Juby near the Village Hall **[The Single Storey building on North Road]**. It was an Independent Chapel. Later funds were raised in 1862 so that a larger more permanent place of worship could

be built on the Yarmouth Road which is now under the denomination of Congregationalists. It had a coach house and stables and a copper house for tea making. As at the beginning of this century the congregation was huge with people (coming) from outlying districts. This chapel was built by John Beech and the Vestry by A.A. Beech both of whom lie there. **[As does George William Beech]** The Chapel was closed in 2009 and opened as Youth Club.

The Methodist Chapel on the corner of Waters Lane and Taylor's Loke (Source Unknown)

The much larger replacement of St. Martin's Chapel (A.J Fakes circa 1985)

St. Martin's Church stood in a large piece of ground opposite the Lacon's Arms in Hemsby Gap. It attracted diminishing congregations and it was decided to sell it. The sale was made around 1960 with a restrictive covenant that it could not be used for "profane" purposes. However, it appears that English Law does not enforce restrictive covenants and it is now Licensed Premises and an Amusement Arcade.

The latest Chapel was a Missionary Church (St. Martins) built of wood, [Pre-War] opposite the Lacon's Arms on the Beach Estate by Messrs Griffin and Anson It has since been demolished. [circa 1970]Pictures supplied by W & H Yallop)

THE PUBS OF HEMSBY

Prior to 1860 anyone could open a beer house and some enterprising people even brewed their own beer. The pleasures of the people were few but at 1½ d or 2d per pint came within the scope of most villagers. Consequently although the population of Hemsby was but 400 in 1845 they managed to maintain six pubs. **[Most of the Holiday Sites have their own licensed 'clubs' today]**.

The only Inn with its peculiar restrictions, licenses and advantages was the 'Blue Bell' subsequently becoming what we now call 'The Norseman'. The original Inn, possibly serving the community for three centuries, was pulled down circa 1912 and was rebuilt being called 'The Bell' and classed as a fully licensed hotel. **[This pub reverted to being called 'The Bell' around 1990.]**

I believe the gentleman seated second on the left is Albert Adrian Beech, George's Father. (Photographs Mrs. P. Long) Michael Allen told me George said that the Bell was built with A.A. Beech's bricks but he was not given the building contract which went to the firm of a Director of Steward & Patterson's Brewery.

John Lovely |**Loveday?**| kept the 'Blue Bell' at the time of the Commons Enclosure ward (1811). Then came John Dyke Cook and Thomas Thurtle took it over in 1845 when the Blue Bell Brewery was bought out by Steward and Patterson in the latter half of Queen Victoria's reign. Albert Thurtle (Known as Knocky) succeeded his father and kept 'The Bell' until 1935. The family having quenched the thirst of the locals for ninety years.

The Bell was refurbished by Watney's as 'The Norseman' for live music performance with side rooms. It was opened at Whitsun 1970 with Ted Fryatt as Manager. It was successful for many years but reverted to being the Bell circa 1990. (Photograph A.J. Fakes.)

The Pub at Newport was called the 'Cliff Inn' and the licence was surrendered in 1914, the last tavern keeper being Jack Lacey. It was used mostly by Coast Guard and Revenue officers, beachcombers and fishermen. 'Fox' Bullock who kept it at the turn of the century was reputed to have given free cod suppers on every Saturday night. Cunning Fox sprinkled the boiled cod heavily with salt, much to the advantage of his exchequer. It eventually became a holiday cottage which it remains today.

Where the row of cottages now stands in Yarmouth Road, there was a yard in the last century containing clay cottages, a chapel and beer house called the 'Trowel and Hammer'. In the High Street what is now Lexington Close [stood] another beer house kept by one named Page.

North Road contained the others - 'The King's Head', no doubt originally a pair of cottages, is there today. Opposite what is now a row of terrace houses built by Jack King was the White House built in 1841 and called the 'Engine Drivers Arms'.

This was well before the Railway came to Hemsby but it could be connected to the steam pump on the Fen which pumped the storm water into Ormesby Broad.

It is peculiar that there now with some 2000 villagers there are but three pubs, all now fully licensed.

'The Lacon Arms' our latest hostelry was built after the style of a Dickensian Posting Inn circa 1934.

[It was designed by A.W. Ecclestone Architect for Lacon's Brewery of Great Yarmouth]

Customers at the King's Head Millie Smith the Landlady is carrying the tray circa 1900.(Unknown Source) Left King's Head circa 1980 (A.J. Fakes)

Post Card of the Lacon's Arms circa 1950. It originally had a fine thatched roof but a disastrous fire on August 12th 1970 burned much of the building. However the bar on the east side of the pub was not damaged and it opened for business on the evening of the fire, referred to as 'Tott's Bar'. Totts was the nickname of Kathleen Hammond who was the barmaid there for many years when Don & Alice Rudrum were mine hosts. A tiled roof replaced the thatch in 1971. It was boarded up and closed in the spring of 2008 but has recently re-opened.

HEMSBY HALL ESTATE

In the latter half of the 18th century, Benjamin Copeman purchased the Manor. It was held by Robert Copeman and lastly by George Barker Copeman (a barrister who never used his talents in court). It had accumulated some 1468 acres, comprising plots of arable land, broad and nine farms (three in Ormesby). They were:-

Meadow Hall Farm (302 acres), Bridge Farm (136 acres), Dairy Barn Farm (98 acres), Common Farm (86 acres), Edmonds Farm (19 acres, Home Farm (170 acres), Decoy Farm (178 acres), Carr Farm (66 acres) and Dunham Farm (90 acres).

The Elms in The High Street, twenty one scattered cottages, The Lodge, seventy seven acres of sand hills also belonged to the estate and a pumping engine to keep the dykes and ditches clear.

Left: This building, on Hemsby Fen housed a coal fired steam pump which carried the water from ditches over a wide area of the parish and sent it into the north east corner of Ormesby Broad. It was demolished around 1980.

Right: This corner of 'Ormesby Broad' lies in the parish of Hemsby. It is now recognized that the Norfolk Broads were formed by the flooding of former peat diggings. E.A. Ellis in his book entitled 'The Broads' (Collins 1965) states that ecclesiastical records show that in Hemsby, tithes worth 15 shillings a year were collected in the late thirteenth and early fourteenth centuries for digging peat. He concludes that about 150,000 turves of peat were dug every year and were taxed as well as those used in the village for heating. Shortly after this time the water levels rose and the diggings were flooded.

Left. North prospect of Hemsby Hall showing Dutch Gables.
Right the grounds of the Hall were sometimes opened up to villagers for fund raising fetes etc.

Above: The south prospect of the hall showing Dutch Gables and well maintained grounds.

Hemsby Hall was built by Robert Copeman in 1868 and superseded the old hall built of white bricks and was roughly on the same site. It consisted of stables and out buildings all with Dutch Gables, as was the Hall which contained sixteen bedrooms, five bathrooms, drawing room, library, dining room, billiard room, gun room, servant's hall, housekeeper's room, butler's pantry, kitchen, scullery, larder and cellars.

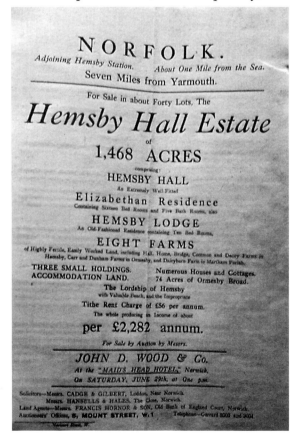

There were wooded coverts nearby, an archery lawn, a market garden, a walled garden and a boathouse; In all 1834 acres.

When Robert Copeman joined his ancestors in Hemsby Church in 1890 the manor reverted to George Barker who didn't seem to appreciate his legacy, for he shot himself in Albert Square in Yarmouth a few years later. His Daughter, Julia Diana Haggard (sister in law of Sir Henry Rider Haggard, the novelist) then inherited the property which she put on the market in 1918. [There is] a brass to the memory of her son, Capt. Mark Haggard in Hemsby Church.

Left: The front page of the catalogue produced around 1918 describing Hemsby Hall estate prior to its disposal. (Mr.Rodney Cook's Collection.)

A shooting party at Hemsby Hall Estate in 1910 for which we have three names. The young man third from left was called 'Podger Myhill and the man third form right is Clem Church. My great grandfather William Fakes (fifth from right with bowler hat and whiskers)

Left: his wife Bertha Fakes nee Beech (she was George Beech's aunt). William was game keeper to Julia Diana Haggard. He was described by my grandmother as 'un-loveable old man' and great deal worse by the rest of the village. He had no compassion for animals and little for human beings. Should he catch a cat in one of his many snares he would strangle it without a second thought. He was cruel to his dogs when they did not obey him. His great zeal to protect Julia Diana's game for shooting did not save him from the sack. She called him in one morning and said "Fakes my good man, I think this estate would be better if it were run by a younger man. Here are your references and notice." He found a job in Essex but later returned to Norfolk to work for Mr. Molineux in Thurne. Grandmother told of an incident when Bertha was returning from Yarmouth on the train. She got off at Potter Heigham Station where William was waiting for her in a rowing boat to return to Thurne. He was 'an impatient old man' and he pushed off when his wife had one foot on the boat and one on the bank. The poor woman more or less somersaulted into the river but was buoyed up by her voluminous clothing. The incident was not good for family harmony. Grandmother said that Bertha was given to alcoholic drink "But being married to that Old Devil it was hardly surprising!" William returned to Hemsby and spent an 'un-conscionable' time dying passing away in Cat's Row in 1928.

Since the demise of the Copemans, the last owners of the Manor never resided in the Hall which was let to various tenants; the last being Mr. Walter Scrimgeour of the stockbroker family then living at Highgate, London. He took on the lease of the Hall from 1908 to 1921 and spent thousands of pounds improving it to his taste. He provided an electric light system as there was no mains electricity here at that time, an improved drainage system, a large dovecote, many more bedrooms because they had a large staff, a billiard room (oak panelled with oak floor and hand built Tudor stove (dog) and oak bookshelves. A pierced stone parapet was built for him in 1914 by A.A. Beech with J Malcolm, his Scottish architect managing the work.

The Hall was the scene of the wedding of Miss Phyllis Scrimgeour to Commander Louis Grieg, Comptroller to the Duke of York who eventually became King George VI. He too visited the Hall.

Hemsby Troop of the Boy Scouts C 1916. George Beech is the third from the right on the top row. The lady in the middle is Miss Phyllis Scrimgeour of the stock broking family.

[In] 1913 Mr. Carron Scrimgeour was married and we, the newly formed Hemsby Troop of Boy Scouts, pulled his car from the Post Office to the Hall, all the drive was being illuminated by fairy lamps. The Scrimgeours left the Hall when their lease was up.

Then in 1925, on being made Lord Mayor of Yarmouth [Yarmouth is not a city so he was only the Mayor] F.F.E. Ferrier who had bought the Hall and sand hills with the title of Lord of the Manor, retired there. They lived there until 1939 when the army requisitioned all the buildings for the duration |of World War II.| Mr. Ferrier having died, Mrs Ferrier and her daughter Judith retired to a house at Blakeney.

The story is in Hemsby that it was the Soldiers billeted there during the Second World War were responsible for the ruin of Hemsby Hall.

Numerous speculators bought the Hall and its grounds and in about 1948 the building was 'cannibalised' to build a smaller structure which has since gone. The plantation of the Home Coverts has since been felled and everything left bare. Many plots from the original land have been built on and occupied. Thus did our stately mansion die.

Incidentally a man was killed while the Hall was being demolished. A large chimney stack fell on a Mr Thurtle, an engineer of Ormesby, when he was standing in the foundations of the building. Funnily enough the tractor was not pulling at it at the time. I wonder if the dead and gone Copemans had a hand in it?

The Ormesby St. Margaret Burial Register no. 748 names him as George Robert Thurtle (age 46) of Westholme, Ormesby (killed in Hemsby). His funeral was on 2nd August 1949. My informant told me that Mr Thurtle had attached a hawser to a gable of the hall and attempted to pull it over with his tractor. As nothing moved he got off the tractor to investigate when the wall collapsed on him.

CATASTROPHES

<u>1870.</u> About 100 years ago, Richard Emmerson a wheelwright, was employed using at that time, an innovation, a circular saw at Hemsby Hall Farm. Inadvertently he felt across the saw bench for a can of oil and off went his right hand! He, afterwards had a hook fitted and could even dig his garden.

<u>1895.</u> The gales of 1895 caused many wrecks at sea and many local fishermen lost their lives or all their belongings when serving with the fishing smacks.

<u>1900+</u> Early in the century the Herring Drifter 'Maggie May' was driven onto a sand bank and floundered. Two brothers called Harbord were lost but John Dyble, hung frozen with cold, in the rigging and was ultimately saved. He lived until a year or so ago.

<u>1908.</u> About 1908 a party of bricklayers and carpenters working at Hemsby Hall for A.A. Beech took a boat and rowed to the Sportsman's Arms on Ormesby Broad. [**The building still stands on the North East corner of the bridge on the A149 Road**]. After getting a skin full, they attempted to row back to Hemsby and, in the ensuing struggle to do so, William Kemp, a carpenter from Southwold was hulled [**hurled**] overboard and drowned.

<u>1912.</u> In [**August**] 1912 East Anglia was flooded [**by heavy rain storms.**] In Hemsby, many trees were brought down including an ash about 80 feet high which badly damaged the stables at Hemsby Hall. I have a chair made from some of this tree.

<u>1920.</u> In the 1920s [**April 1922**] a boy named Jimmy Knights [**Leonard James Knights**] of Dow Hill Hemsby was killed by a train as he played on the embankment of the Yarmouth Road Bridge. The [**strong**] wind hindered him from hearing the approach of the train. At the inquest the engine driver said he was unaware of the collision. (Yarmouth Mercury).

Mrs Ida Horsham told me she remembered him as a bright boy who would probably have gone on to Grammar School

The Railway Bridge carried the Midland & Great Northern Joint Line over the main B1159, Yarmouth Road through Hemsby where Jimmy Knights died. It stood near the junction of Newport Road and the Main Yarmouth Road. It was difficult for drivers to see if any vehicles were coming from under the bridge resulting in several crashes. Mr Tom Bammant Junior lived at Newport Farm and did not want to go all the way to Hemsby Station and would jump from the moving train near this bridge using his paratroops' training. I am also told that a double deck bus was wedged under the bridge and had to have its tyres deflated before it could be released. It was dismantled during the 1960s and the main road ran along the old railway line so that traffic going north no longer had to go through Hemsby Street. (Mrs. R Shepheard's Collection)

1928. The grandfather of our present butcher, Mr. Clifford Allen was driving on the Caister Road during a thunderstorm some fifty years ago, and the storm broke down the electric cable supplying the trams with power and fell on the pony which was electrocuted. Mr Allen and his wife, thanks to providence were thrown clear.

1939. In an electric thunderstorm many buildings were struck by lightning.

1940-. During the war a little girl stepped on a mine and was killed. **[See section on Second World War.]**

1960-. The Lacon's Arms **[Pub]** was badly damaged by fire in the 1960s. **[Actually 12th August 1970.]** The Games Hall at Maddieson's Camp was destroyed by fire just after the last war.

January 31ˢᵗ 1950. It was quickly rebuilt by Mr. Jimmy Brown of the Martham Boat Building Company with some difficulty as building materials were in short supply just after they were able to open for the holiday season.

THE TWO GREAT WARS

I shall not dwell on the war years in the History of Hemsby because those eleven years which were taken from our normal lives were experienced by countless thousands on this island. Those eleven years of apprehension, semi-starvation, worry for those on the battlefield and on the sea. Watching in the cold under searchlights, crawling in and out of dug-outs and straw will be better relegated to a limbo and forgotten, but in our hearts we cannot forget.

Ada Elizabeth and Arthur Johnson Fakes who was fortunate enough to survive the First World War and rose to the rank of sergeant in the Royal Artillery. The only picture I have of a Hemsby man killed in WWI is believed to be of Frank 'Chummy' Allen cousin of the Butcher Harry Allen. He was 'killed in action' 22/3/1918 and has no known grave.

The 'do your own thing' generations of the post war should get down and thank God they were not brought up in times of relative peace and be truly thankful.

Some 200 men joined up in the First War and twenty lost their lives.

George Turner won the Military Medal and the Croix de Guerre, In the first few weeks nearly all single men joined Kitchener's Army and were decimated at Loos the following year. Many local fishermen lost their lives in the Royal Naval Volunteer Reserve while mine sweeping.

From 1915 we were protected by the 16th Norfolk Cycle Battalion who patrolled the Norfolk Coast as they also did 1939-40. In 1916, invasion was in the official mind and there was a Brigade Headquarters at North Walsham consisting of the 4th Monmouth Regiment, the 22nd Cheshire Regiment, 23rd Royal Welsh Fusiliers and the 49th Provisional Battalion mostly Lancashire troops.

In 1916 the valley and trenches [?] were bivouacked, the 29th Argyle and Sutherland Highlanders, who eventually sent most drafts to the front. 1800 men, with bagpipes and drums leading used to march to the church. A noble sight.

There was a battery of R.F.A. [Royal Fleet Auxiliary?] at Newport. The Hollies (The Old Manor House) was the headquarters of the 49th Provisional Battalion and later the 14th South Lancs. and by 1919 the 23rd Royal Welsh Fusiliers sent companies to Horsey, Winterton, Hemsby Beach, Martham, Scratby and Rollesby.

The public took little interest in air bombing in the first war and no one thought of dug-outs, all were in the open then to watch the Zeppelins and the anti aircraft guns firing at them.

How different in 1940-44! Newport people were lucky to have had no casualties in 1943, when a squadron of Focke Wulfs attacked the village with bombs and cannon fire. Their leader (a Knight Commander of Oak Leaves) hit a pylon behind Newport Cottages. The collision drove him into his instruments and killed him. His plane, travelling at enormous speed, jumped over the houses and plunged into the sea.

Yarmouth, officially named as the most bombed port on the East Coast, was visited by 'Jerry' every fine day and of course by the same planes. You could set your watch by them.

[I think this is exaggerated. If it was so fighters would be waiting for them.]

A land-mine was dropped in North Road in 1943 [19th March] caused demolition and damage to 98 houses. (See the section on the Second World War in Hemsby.)

THE DEVELOPMENT OF HEMSBY

As the 20th century opened, this village was already getting known as a holiday resort as the thousands of young Londoners, who were catered for by Joe Powell of the Garibaldi Hotel in Great Yarmouth, locally referred to as 'Powell's Lambs' because they were polite and well behaved, used to hire horse drawn brakes to visit the surrounding countryside and pubs. Those people on returning home, told friend and neighbour who eventually tried the ozone of Hemsby. By 1906, all suitable houses in the village were taking in families, mostly 'professional class' Londoners for two or three week summer holidays and Hemsby's fame snowballed.

There were some people who looked ahead, and in 1904, the Hemsby Beach Estate, adjoining Beach Road and the sand hills was laid out with named roads. The plots were staked and numbered by A.A. Beech for the new owners. People from far away were encouraged to buy sites and build their summer homes.

Very few visitors of the artisan or working class took their holidays here at that time but just before the Great War , John Fletcher Dodd opened a Socialist **[and temperance]** Holiday Camp at Caister to cater for that need.

ENTRANCE TO HEMSBY HOLIDAY CAMP.

BATHING POOL, MADDIESONS HEMSBY HOLIDAY CAMP

Hemsby Holiday Camp on the south side of Beach Road. For many years it was referred to as Maddieson's Camp. David Tubby's (Collection)

The First World War came and stagnated all such projects, but in 1920 the Brothers Potter, well known in Norwich for their association with bell ringing at St Peter Mancroft Church, bought land on the North side of Beach Road and built a holiday camp. But, subject to a clause in the deeds they were stopped from running a business there. So they bought the area bounded by Back Market Lane, Beach Road and the railway line. After several years the brothers parted and Mr. H.J (Harry) Maddieson bought the camp.

HMY. 42   The Valley, Newport, Near Hemsby.

It briefly became an 'International Youth Camp' but became Hemsby Holiday Village under the Pontin's name and took its last visitors in 2008

The bungalow on the left was owned by Mr Bertie Frost of Blofield. He was a delivery man and manager for International Stores in Norwich. He was said to have lined this building with recycled tea chests.

In 1930 the Yarmouth butchers, W.I. Bishop and Sons, who lived in King's Loke used the land adjoining and opened 'Seacroft' Holiday Camp which has entertained thousands of visitors each year up the present time, excepting the war years when both camps were used by the army.

Above: Campers at Seacroft.

Mr Jack Bishop proprietor of Seacroft. He became the first Mayor of Great Yarmouth Borough Council when Yarmouth and the Fleggs were amalgamated as a unit of local government in 1974.

Above: a picture of the original buildings let to holiday makers. Fortunately they were not used when there was snow on the ground. (Source of photographs unknown)

Seacroft Camp was purchased by Pontins in 1974 and taken over by Richardson's of Stalham around 2000.

Albert Stanley Olley opened a shop and pioneered amusement arcades at Hemsby Gap. It was literally a penny arcade with mechanical machines but with bright electric lights. It was possible to flick a lever and a 'silver' ball bearing would go round and should it go in the right hole a money prize would be released.

He was prosecuted in 1948 for having machines which were said to be games of chance rather than games of skill. But as he reasonably told the court he had been operating since 1924 and the police had visited the premises every year without complaint before the war he had assumed all was well. Albert paid £6:16:6d costs and agreed to destroy the offending machines and the case was dismissed (Yarmouth Mercury).

The beach and sand hills at Hemsby built up before 1980 with new sand and stones washing up on the shoreline from further north. However, the sand banks in the North Sea moved. This forced a 'rip' tide on to the coast at Hemsby which carried a great deal of sand away, undermining the dunes and the bungalows on the beach and on top of the hill fell down or were pulled down in spite of heroic efforts to save them. All these properties had gone by the mid 1990s.

However, subsequently sites were let on the sand hills by the Lord of the Manor (R.F.E. Ferrier Esq.) for beach bungalows and many villagers got on the band wagon until most of the dunes were covered.

These were the last words written by George Beech in his History of Hemsby on Sea. It did not have a conclusion or a summary. I believe that he was keen to see it published in his life-time, hence the brisk ending.

OLD NORFOLK HOUSEN

George Beech wrote this article in 1975 when he heard that certain nonagenarians (90 year olds). were living in accommodation unfit for human habitation. George had known many people who had survived perfectly well in similar or worse conditions than those discussed. He therefore wrote this description of building and living in the older type of house, He used the word "Housen" which he felt was the old English plural of house just as oxen is the plural of ox,

He passed this article to his friend Mr. Alec McEwen who was a member of Great Yarmouth and District Archaeological Society. The article was published posthumously in the Society's Annual Journal 'Yarmouth Archaeology' in 1993. It sets out George's thoughts and memories, on house construction the building trade and general living conditions. It seems to say that things were better in the past which was his opinion; but running water, indoor flush toilets, houses that are largely draft free and warm, without the trouble of open fires and flame based lighting are things that I, for one, would be sorry not to have. George's living conditions were similar to those of 100 years ago but they seemed to please him and, as he said, people lived for a long time in those conditions. He may have been right in as much modern living conditions are said to give rise to allergies, asthma and general ill health.

This picture shows Mr. Jimmy Jones, Baker of Winterton and his wife outside the cottages on North Road. The walls are built of un-knapped beach stones with brick lintels and corners and these materials could be 'sourced' locally. (Source of picture, unknown)

Before the advent of the railways, transport was a very precarious business for any quantity of material over a large area; hence in the centuries up to the industrial revolution, people had to use material for building that grew on the spot. We know, of course, that Caen stone was imported (with the masons) when cathedrals and churches were rushed up by the Crusaders, thanking God that they had escaped the scimitars of the Saracens or eternal slavery, stone came by sea into the many small ports of the East coast.

Much of the church building took place shortly after the Norman Conquest or later by rich nobles, merchants and clerics worried that they would not get into heaven whereas the Crusaders had been told their sins were pardoned by their taking up arms against the Saracens but they may well have been thankful to have survived. There was a further boom in Church building in the later Middle Ages based on agricultural wealth.

George Beech's 'Print Shop' an example of 'Clay Lump' and various other types of building with proverbial 'Brick Privy'. (M. Pickard c 1970)

Norfolk cottages of the 17th - 19th centuries can be divided into two classes, both using local materials. Clay and pebble work, not to be confused with flint, which meant knapped or squared stone. A land owner with a few pounds to lay out, would build a terrace of cottages for fishermen or farm workers. For small houses there was no form of contracting as we later knew it. He would ask a bricklayer for a price to run up the building, plaster inside and lay the floor bricks. A carpenter to pitch the roof and make a few casements and doors. A tiler or thatcher to finish the roof. The house could be built for about £5. He bought a few bricks for quoins and binders. The pebbles came from the beach free, all but the cost of carting sand free. Main timber from shipwrecks.

Clay housen were built from sun dried blocks tied with straw or foul grass, and laid with clay joints. Alternatively the walls were 'splant work', an approximate sized frame of poles about 2 inches thick , tied with tarred spun yarn and then plastered all round the frame about a foot thick with clay mixed with foul grass. It was laid with a tool that had two flat prongs. They laid a foot a day all round the building, ruled it upright as in plastering and let it harden. My father, who started in the building trade at the age of nine, said that he had only been on one job in his life laying clay walls and it was harder work than making up concrete. Inner walls were brick or pebble laid with clay. The foundations (damp course as we know it, didn't exist) were a foot or more of pebbles laid in stone lime, a pretty good damp course.

Unknown elderly couple who I believe lived in Pit Road. The bricks look larger than normal. I wonder how old these people were? (Source of picture, unknown.)

Clay walls were treated when dry with distemper made of stone lime (coming up a cream colour) and in-side lime putty whitewash. Floors were invariably brimstone bricks bedded on sand. These were not joined in any way, but after being laid, sand was brushed into all open joints. When worn in places, the floor bricks were turned over and re-bedded. They were pretty hard wearing being made from loam. These are not to be confused with pammens which were generally black or red Staffordshire clay. The windows generally in cottages were casements composed of many small panes. While today people use enormous panes in their windows, our grandfathers saved money and eyesight with small panes which diffuse the light. The glass had a pinkish tone.

Roofs were either red or smut pan tiles, which would last a very long time against the weather, or they were thatched, possibly the oldest form of roof cladding.

Norfolk reed is sold in bunches about six inches across and they used to sell it by the fathom (as many bunches as could be placed in a six foot circle. The thatcher would lie on his sloping ladder outside, and the boy crawled on a deal on the joists inside. He threaded a long needle with tarred spun yarn (in ancient times they used brambles) which the thatcher pushed through to run on the side of [the] spar; it was passed round the reed on the other side of the spar and the boy tied a knot. The thatcher dressed the roof, verges and drips of the dormer windows with his block of wood filled with horse shoe nails which acted as both a mallet and a rake.

Although Norfolk people at this time were taller than those from some counties, they nearly always made their bedrooms so they could not stand upright. In many houses the spars came down to the floor with just a bit of ceiling in the middle. Upper floors were jointed wide boards, spruce or chestnut, and rose headed nails. The ground floor of brick was sanded every day afresh, unless the inmate could afford "sale" a kind of linoleum.

The layout of cottages followed a universal pattern. For this type of house, kitchen and front room, which was later called the parlour and only used for Christmas, weddings or funerals (when the family would dab their noses with black edged handkerchiefs as they walked round the en-coffined dead, munching seed cake and sipping glasses of Burgundy.) If the squire or Parson called, they might be invited into the parlour, otherwise it was forbidden.

The kitchen or living room followed a general pattern. From the back with the fireplace in the middle, one started with the "chamber" (bedroom) door opening on the winder stair well (which was about three of four feet only,) and much more economical of space than a straight flight, riser and treads of fir or elm notched or birds mouthed in to a rebated newel post on side and housed into the brickwork on the other. I would imagine they were "built by eye."

Next came the brick oven or perhaps an iron "Perpetual" oven about three or four feet from the floor, whose flue ran into the main chimney which either supported a range or hob stove with "hake [hook] and chain" built over it to hold iron pots. By the way, chimney flues were 'parged' [plastered] with mortar and cow dung inside as they were built and this took some burning out. Some of the old chimneys were very wide and tapered with long spikes knocked in here and there with long spikes for the boys to stand on when sent up to sweep it. Next in this partition we find a narrow cupboard for storing dry clean sand to sprinkle on the floor. After this was a two storey cupboard perhaps four feet wide for a general store.

They were snug old kitchens. There would have been a 'Beaufort' or corner cupboard, farmhouse "stick" chairs, Windsors or chairs with dished seats of thin oak which children had a job to settle on, a deal kitchen table with drawers for cutlery, a warming pan, a settle to stand the newly baked loaves and cakes on. Upstairs, one would find a profusion of religious texts, one or two oleographs, a four poster bed with its damask roof and curtains and two little pockets sewn into the head to put watches. Possibly a bow-fronted chest of drawers, but generally chests covered with cretonne with valance edges, held people's wearing apparel. Some of these had an inner box with a drawer and a lid pivoted into the sides of the chest which had an individual lock. In many fisherman's cottages I have seen painted glass rolling pins on a cord over the doorways. These originally contained gin which crews of the smacks had brought from the Dutch bum boats out at sea. They "lowered" the gin and brought the pretty containers home for their families. Some cottages had small bedrooms butted on to the main house for the children. These were invariably a step lower than the main bedroom. If there was only one large bedroom, half of it was parted by stalls for the children with a passage near the foot of the bed into the larger bedroom but no doors. Victorian circumspection forbade children from sleeping with their parents and thus learning the means of their own introduction to this naughty world. Our sanctimonious forbears were anything if not cunning.

Outside would be a wash house with a "coal shed" containing a copper and its flue, a tub, a scrubbing board and a wicker linen basket. The remaining adjunct would be the "petty" or earth closet, which today is looked upon as very barbaric, but in my experience is much less repulsive to the nose than the eventual closets with sanitary pails, because the layers of cinders put into the former nullified the smell. Even the nobility of the 18th century just sprinkled their fair limbs with powder and scent rather than washing. In this present age, we have "experts"on every conceivable subject , falling over themselves to tell us that the old clay cottages were "Quite picturesque but totally unhealthy and unsanitary". When I remember the octogenarians and nonagenarians that I knew as a boy who were reared, lived and died in such homes, I can only say "All theorists". My experience is that provided the clay housen were completely dried out before decorating , the rain and frost kept from entering the walls and the thatch kept free from rats and birds , clay houses were an advance on brick because they were cool in summer and warm in winter. Birds could play havoc in the thatch. Rats could leave little friends [fleas] among the reeds, and as the ceilings were also reed, covered with "hair mortar", these parasites had a good home. I remember when we were re-plastering a farm house where the ceilings ran down to the floor as the spars went, so we had to kneel or lie flat to trowel the bottom and when we tore down the old reed ceiling, the same friends of the rats really invaded us, like ants in the primeval forests, they tried to eat us alive. One can still hear the hoarse shouts of the plasterers, and the curses as we retreated preparatory to smoking the rooms with burnt sulphur.

One could knock a hole through nine inch brick work much quicker than a twelve inch clay wall. I have found poles of elm and oak in old clay lump walls which sprang up when hit by an axe. Others were just bark and dust in the same wall. I have a knobbed stick which I took from a clay wall forty years ago, it having been confined in the clay for perhaps 500 years. Also a piece of 16th century oak scratch moulding found recently between two walls in an old cottage.

As for brick and stone housen, in this area clay can be dug at about two feet, and several of our canny predecessors dug clay from their sites and burnt enough bricks there from for their houses. These were very inferior bricks for two reasons (a) good bricks can only be made from "brick earth", a special clay (b) they were not burnt in a kiln with regulated draught [?] but in a "clamp" which is a layer of " green" bricks and a layer of small coal all of which was set alight. Most of the bricks would be mottled; some would have had a purple colour having practically fused. These would not worked well on the line, however they would bond to pebbles.

G .W. Beech 1975.

FROM "NORFOLK MEDLEY"
BY RUSTICUS
The Flegg Press Hemsby MCMXL1 (1941)

Although I had heard of this book before, I had not seen it until Mr. Jack Durrant let me look at his copy. I feel it gives a further insight into the character of George Beech who as the author calls himself Rusticus being the Latin for A Countryman.

He had heard many stories probably from local pubs and he took the trouble to write them down over sixty years ago. Of course some are more successful than others and I reproduce a few of them. These stories and poems allow George to be satirical, mocking and sarcastic about fellow Hemsby people and are probably more interesting for that. The poetry is not always successful because though George's sense of rhyme is good the metre of the poems let him down occasionally.

TO THE CRITICAL READER.

In placing this small volume before you I fulfill an ambition -to emulate Caxton and write something, print it and bind it.

Also as a native of the 'King's County' I feel that Norfolk has been sadly neglected as a subject for novels, while some counties have been overdone by our talented writers.

I am well aware of the amateurishness of my first literary attempt; by your helpful criticism future work may be much improved.

Let me apologise for introducing a modicum of bad language herein, but to leave it out or substitute asterisks would spoil the yarns for it is the chutney with the cold pork (shades of Lord Woolton) as it were. Norfolk humour lacks the sparkling wit of the Cockney, but its very dryness makes it rich.

Now, I fade into the background while you have a good laugh -- if you do, then my book has fulfilled its mission and fame is in the offing.

RUSTICUS.

* * *

THE WITCHING HOUR
An Adventure in Norfolk
By Rusticus

Note by AJF. Although the following story may seem a bit dated it was written in 1941 by a man who had no contact with many of the books, radio and television programmes we have today. I wonder how original the plot is but all Shakespeare's plots were borrowed, and like Shakespeare George had an extensive vocabulary which he was keen to show off.

It has only been recently that the Norfolk accent has been analysed properly and I feel George would have been a keen supporter of F.O.N.D. (Friends of the Norfolk Dialect). Not everything that is spoken supposedly in a Norfolk accent is good but the true Norfolk accent is like beauty; easy to recognize but difficult to define.

George was doing his best to write in the Norfolk dialect though I think he misses an important distinguishing features of it; that is the "i" sound in such words as night, tight and time becomes 'oi' in Norfolk 'noigth' 'toight' and 'toime'. I confess I'm a bit uneasy about George's spelling of the word 'you' as 'yow'. This sounds like they might pronounce it in the Midlands. I feel that a Norfolk person would pronounce the word as though it were spelt 'yew'. However, I note too that Sidney Grapes 'The Boy John', Potter Heigham Correspondent of the Eastern Daily Press 1946 -1958 uses the same spelling as George.

The Sexton, Brown, in this story 'The Witching Hour' is clearly based on Little Dick Gowen (pronounced in Hemsby, 'Gown').I believe Dick was like Sam Weller in 'The Pickwick Papers' and his Vs became Ws. The Vicar would have been the Reverend Basil Gordon Dunthorne Clarke M.A. (Durham) who I remember as a genial old gent with a bald pate and white hair. He walked with a stick and constantly visited around the parish, but I am told that he was a good athlete and rugby player in his youth. I take it the rest is a satire and the three villains are based on known Hemsby characters. George mentions the town of Yareham which must be Yarmouth. The geography of his village is the same as Hemsby with the Hotel, the Grocer and the Butcher being near the Church. So I suspect he is using the well known cinema trick of 'only changing the names to protect the innocent'.

Hemsby Church men's group circa 1950 shows the Reverend Basil Clarke second from the left seated (Peter Matthews Collection) The picture of interior of the church is undated but as there seems to be electricity in use it must be after 1929

Chapter 1

It was almost midnight, the Vicar glanced at the marble clock on his study mantelpiece. Yes, he must soon retire. Why wouldn't ideas come for his sermon?

He had scanned his subjects - Love, Honesty, Humility, Humanity, Obedience - he'd worked all these themes threadbare. What about Gratitude? Ah, Gratitude, that would be it. Now to work.

He soliloquized 'Possibly that excellent, pious Church-goer of last Sunday will take my tip, after this discourse on Gratitude, and make a more useful and substantial donation to the offering than the ten centime I found in the bag after that service'

Our Parson mused, "How little their souls are worth, how little they appreciate the Goodness of Providence." Still it wasn't for him to judge; his rubicund countenance lit up with a beatific smile. "I too, am a sinn-" he started to remark, but paused aghast.

The Vicar blanched beneath his tan, for he had seen, but a moment before, a grotesque shadow pass by his curtained window, a form resembling nothing he knew, unless it was the 'Hunchback of Notre Dame' he had viewed at the Yareham Kinema.

"What could it mean?" he pondered.

Although an Apostle of Peace, he must investigate… precious lives were in his charge. Feeling none too belligerent, he arose, threw his half smoked cigar into the pentray, and grinding his fountain-pen into the lovely Axminster carpet, he prepared to reconnoitre.

As he entered the hall, and grasped the main door handle, he perceived this self-same apparition coming up the steps towards him. Seizing a silver mounted shillelagh, (presented to him by members of the Lonely Mothers' Needle-work Guild in his last parish, he threw open the heavy door, at the same time exclaiming, in the most terrible tones he could muster. "My dear good man, what can you possibly require at this late hour?"

The man, or pseudo-hunchback paused in his stride, threw from his shoulder the bag of coke which made him appear to be so afflicted and answered "Why Wicar, yow wouldn't smoke inta me, wouldja?"

"Well to be sure its Brown, the Sexton," said our vicar, greatly relieved. "How you startled me, Brown. Whatever can be your business at this-er-unearthly hour, my good fellow?"

"I'm werry sorry to distarb yow, Wicar, at this time 'o night, but I hed tu," replied the Sexton . "Ya see, I was a kerryin' this here coke inta the charchya'd to light the stuk-hole fire, when I heered some lot of duller [noise] comin' from there, tu or three mens's woices a'talking loud; bein' a little man. I run arter yow direck'ly, so I hope yow'll axcuse me?"

"Of course, of course, Brown," replied the Parson, "I think we will investigate. We will institute a search immediately. What shall I provide as weapon for you?"

The Sexton coughed spasmodically and answered "Yow doan wanna git noffin for me sir; spuzzin the warst come to the warst I c'n hull [hurl] this here bayg o' coke down on the warmin! [vermin"]

"Ah yes, to be sure," said the Vicar, "Let us adopt some tactics, Brown. Er --you had best creep round the west side, while I, myself will reconnoiter the east, and so come on the miscreants, unawares."

Brown staggered off with his projectile, whilst our parson strolled to his appointed post, musing the while, "By St. Francis of Assisi this is a rum business! To be groping around a graveyard like ghouls, in the middle of the night!"

Chapter 2

The Village was stilled. The neighbouring grocer had long since turned off his 'McMurphy' nine valve [radio, or as the author would have said "wireless".] and crept under the eiderdown; the milk man just yawned, turned in his sleep and wondered if it were time to milk; the butchers nearby were snoring in unison with their pigs, and all the hotel lights had disappeared, now that pots and glasses had been washed up ready for the morning callers.

Unaware of the approach of our vigilantes down in the stoke-hole sprawled three men, crouching as best they could in such an uncomfortable shelter. One was a short bearded fellow, with dirty fair hair, and his face reddened by exposure, or perhaps by a steady application of the flowing bowl. He had on an old army great-coat, three sizes too large as a top dressing; as most of the buttons had gone, he had to rely on a thin piece of rope to make the coat fit him. His partner on the right was a tall, raw boned cadaverous individual, with matted black hair surmounted by a blue cap lodged over one ear; a man who talked as little as possible. The remaining villain was also tall; was younger, with a much better appearance than either of the former.

He it was who remarked "I gorra spaed."

The short man growled "I thought there was a blinker about somewhere. What ha' yow got Jack?" to the morose fellow.

"I think I c'n do har with a club," replied he. "Afore ya do," said the first "I'll yoke har, she oon't stand thet!"

"Good Heavens!" thought the Vicar, who had neared the cubby-hole, "It's Murder-- they have weapons, and spades to cover all traces. What better place could they find than here. I buried old Sam Lown only this afternoon, and it wouldn't be noticed if the fresh soil were again disturbed."

He knelt down and peered through a tiny crack in the boarded lid, but could only get a vague impression of the interior, as it was but lighted by the glow of their pipes.

"A more murderous trio it would be hard to find," thought he.

"Draw for't," said the man of few words. "Don't arger on a night like this."

The younger one retorted, "Yow want all the jam; ye'r bound to draw the Ole Lady, du yow wouldn't be so eager!"

"Old Lady," mused the watcher - "So that is their project."

He had often heard a whisper that on old women who lived close at hand, the relict of a farmer who had been worried into his grave by the Pig Board, the Milk Board and the Potato Board, was reputed to be a very rich miser, as many people living alone in the country are believed to be - so she was to be their victim!

He grasped his stout stick, and, although his hair was lifting his clerical hat every now and then, he was determined, although ostensibly a non-combatant, to battle for the weak as behoved a Minister of the Church.

The morose man was heard to say "Time we started, boys,"

"Yis," said the first culprit, "Less git our gear tagedder. I'm damn frozen bein' in here."

They all grabbed what appeared to be their weapons and grouped for the step-ladder.

The Sexton, who had been kneeling all the time, frightened, on the opposite side of the hatch top and had also been looking through a small hole in it, could contain himself no longer. The rank smoke of their pipes had percolated through into his hyper-sensitive throat, so he let out a loud wheeze like an Irish Banshee.

"What the hell d'ya reckon thet wus?" asked the youngest villain starting up.

"Ghuss!" **[Ghosts]** answered the morose one- "If I'd 'a known, yow wouldn't a ligged me inta no charchya'ds; I tell ya we oughter met some other place."

"Did ya want the pleece **[police]** a foul on us yow fule," said the fair man- "I naver thought we'd a got disturbed in these quarters, I c'n tell ya , 'specially by Ghuss!."

"I'm outa this, ghuss whether-or-no," shouted the young man. "they aren't a goin to smuthercate me down here if I c'n help it; our gaem is done f'r tonight- tha's a proper 'Blue Light' now. Outa the way all on ya!"

He sprang up the steps and flung open the trap-door. This was done so suddenly and violently, that it threw both the Parson and the Sexton off their equilibrium and deposited them on some mounds several yards away.

The rest of the assassins quickly followed their leader and made off as fast as they could, over the boundary wall and the night swallowed them up.

Our Vicar regained his poise; picked up his clerk, after first disentangling him from the sack of coke and exclaimed "Brown, my dear good man, what pawns we are in the Great Game of Life! We have saved a life this night. We have prevented the ghastly murder of a defenceless old woman."

"Marder Raverint Sir?" Wot the dev… I mean wotavver a' yow a sayin on?" said the Sexton mystified.

"Didn't you hear those villains discussing who was to tie up the old lady and who should wield the club?" asked the Vicar in a somewhat stern manner.

The other coughed reluctantly and replied dryly "Lor bless ya. Sir, things worn't krite ez bed ez yow reckon; I seed wot they were a doin on, but dussent [dare not] spake t'ya. They war a playing 'Joker'. A gambling' outa the way o' the pleece, an the 'ole lady' was the Queen of Hearts-an' not a proper woman."

They struck a match and looked down- scattered all over the boiler and floor was a pack of cards.

"And to think that I might have been in the arms of Morpheus, instead of shivering here!" sadly spoke the Vicar as he moved homeward.

"I don't hold wiv furrin names f'r wimmen," muttered Brown the Sexton as he descended into Avernus*

*I find from my Dictionary of Phrase and Fable that Avernus is used by Latin writers to describe the entrance to the underworld or the underworld itself.

SAGA OF THE DUNES

[George's 'Purple Passages' relates to an imagined 'Viking Raid' with some inconsistencies.]

I had strolled to the beach, to see about some repairs to a bungalow standing in the hamlet of 'Newby' It was rather a long walk on a sultry June evening, so after doing business I lay on the marram covered hill and gazed out to sea, intrigued by the many small 'long-shore' boats herring fishing [possibly not herrings in June] under the moon.

Some men were on the foreshore, bending? nets preparatory to 'going off'. I looked in their direction; and then I saw her.

Lithesome and strong , with her rounded cream arms bare to the sun, and her golden tresses falling in an abundant 'bob' on her fair neck, she walked un-falteringly down the sloping path in the sand hills that led from the hamlet above, to a beached boat; her blue eyes searching the horizon.

My glanced followed this Aurora, and even as it dwelt on her the bungalows were engulfed by the marram; the fishing boats took on a longer shape; the bows turned to tall prows rudely carved; nets to shields.

The men's Jerseys had disappeared, leaving in their place home-spun blouses with runic decorations, surmounted by bear-skins, caps changed to horned casques;

Horned helmets were not worn by Vikings of the 8th - 11th centuries in spite of many illustrations to the contrary dating back to Victorian historians.

Grey flannels had given place to raw- hide lashed hose - in short the ancestors of the sturdy Newby men, the Jomsborg Vikings were re-incarnated in them.

The maiden's bobbed hair became four golden plaits, crowned by a narrow brass circlet, and reaching her knees. Her dress, changed to Norse kjortel, was white with a cornflower-blue runic edge, neatly covering her bare feet.

Maren Trygveson!

Her bare arm swept toward the sea to the black dots that were cresting the waves and getting bigger as they neared the shore.

She turned to one of the men; one whose tanned features seem to have been hewn from red granite, and whose unkempt tawny hair greying. "Father," said she, "Yonder come the men of Hardangerfjord; the cruel Erik Thorvold is at the helm of his serpent."

"They come to harry our quiet kinsmen and burn our wheaten store; even to carry thine undutiful daughter to an ill-omened 'By' in the North."

"Fly to thine arms; do not tarry, thou men of Ulfkel Snilling. I will awaken the By - else all is lost.

She unhooked from her ornamented girdle a small white horn, and blew it.

The men, who came running from everywhere, brandishing their broad-swords and stringing their bows, all grouped themselves around her father. Then lead us, Trygve Olafson" they cried, "Lead us against the cursed despoilers of all that is dear to us."

He drew himself up to his full two ells, and answered, "'tis well ye have chosen me, the son of Olaf, for in my youthful days, I too, foraged with those of the Vik, and know their battle cunning. By the bloody hammer of Thor shall we lay them low in the water's rim, and they shall be made the 'bloody eagles' on our strand.

Vikings were reputed to open up the chest cavities of their victims and fold the flesh back ripping the living heart out, The remains of the person was supposed to look like an eagle This would 'discourage the others'

Ride thou then Einar Thorkelson to the By of Hem and bid the good men or Thorveir Ormsgard hasten hither swift as the wind.

The great galleys had neared the beach, and as they grounded some two hundred wild, hardy Viking leaped over the shield bedecked bulwarks, on to the yielding sand.

"By the Great Goat of Odin, ye are doomed" they shouted , "Fall down , ye tillers of the red earth, ye are no men of valour - thy swords have rusted through ill use; go to thy byres and thy barley fields, ye are no match for free rovers of the sea. Thy kine and maidens shall go to our households in the frozen North.

The tide of battle ebbed and flowed like the blue green sea that enfiladed them.

A swift advance; the twang of bow and the thud of arrows; the clash of swords on shields; a groan from many a prostrate figure; shouted oaths; reddened sand .

The tumult became quieter, the seething mass less tangled. I saw a vision of the Norse girl bending over the stricken form of Trygve Olafson.

"My father" she cried "Say thou art not dying. Our foeman that are not slain have been driven into the maw of the sea.

I will hasten forthwith and get thee linen and salve to stem thy wound,"

He muttered "Maren dearest, grieve not thou for me; I shall recover anon. Valhalla is not for me yet."

The maid turned and ascended the hill.

I felt a twinge in my ankle which awaked me, and heard a quiet Norfolk voice saying "Oh, I am sorry, Mister, jamming' on ya like thet - I didn't see ya in the merrum; I was a bit worried ez my father a bin taken quare, an' I'm jest a' gorn to git him suffin' to drink. I think the heat got hold on him"

It was May, the Newby fishermen's lass with a look of pain in her cornflower-blue eyes.

[When the story began it was June]

EAST NORFOK HUMOUR

MAROONED IN GRIMSBY

This seems to be an anecdote that George has been told by the 'Hero' of the story. Truly 'an Epic Binge Drinker'

Christmas, an old fashioned fisherman was recalling the days when one started at the tender age of nine in the old sailing smacks - when every skipper was judge, jury and especially - executioner aboard. When they were 'wooden ships and iron men' instead of today's 'iron ships and wooden men.'

"Ah!" he said "they war the times! We di'nt live in ------palaces wi brass rails and baths aboard, like now-a-days.

I remember jamming' **[walking]** right ta Grimsba (Grimsby) one time, arter a ship. I gorra barth on the Iceland Woyage , so when I come home I had plenty of clink **[cash]** ta teke.

I wus strollin' along o' the quay when I heered a lot of duller comin' of a wessel tied up along-aside; so I clambered aboard .

Wha' d'ya think I see? - go to hell if there worn't a couple of furriners a settin on the breedge **[foreigners sitting on the bridge]** waving a bottle of grog in thar hends; both on 'em war three sheets at the wind, an' when I come agin 'em , one on 'em hallered to me ' I'll kill yow b----- Englishman!' They war furriners ; b----- Australians !"

I said "No yow dam-well oont, an afore they c'd do anything I snetched the bottles out of their hends , an' cracked buth on 'em on the skull with 'em , and jumped ashore.

79

A long while arter, I wuk up alonga a lot more chaps, in a big room. I looked round an' say at one on 'em 'Where the devil ha' I got to mate?' an' he say 'Doan cha know where you are, chap?'- y're in Chookey **[Gaol]**.

An' so I was. I'd drunk the two bottles o' rum, an' they found me asleep an' run me in . Arter a day or two they pulled me a' front o' the ole beak, an' he snared et me an say 'Prisoner, yow a' fined two guineas or hetta teke seven day f'r bein' drunk an dis-orderla in the High Street.'

I say at him 'I'll hetta teke the time, Yar Warship'cus I hint got no money'

There wus a rozzer **[policeman]** agin me an' he say, 'Yis you hev Christmas, when we searched yow , yow had tree pound fifteen on ya, so yow ken pay the fine an' then hev enow left over at git canned agin!'

"And a funny thing" continued the old salt, "An so I did the werry next day.

The Yarmouth Steam Drifter Ivy YH796. Men from the Fleggs could sign on as ship's crew in the Herring season which lasted from September to November and other 'berths' were available in ships for those prepared to travel.

TERROR ON THE DUNES

A visitor was lounging in the tap-room in a neighbouring fishing village.

Having to while away some minutes before his conveyance arrived and, knowing that fishermen are proverbially superstitious, he casually remarked to one of the assembly, "got any ghosts about these parts, boy?"

Looking the enquirer up and down to see if he was leg pulling, he at length answered "Tu or tree, Mister."

"Tell me about them, will you? And also have a drink with me for your trouble" said the stranger.

The man drained his pot, handed it over the counter for a refill and commenced.

"Well the one we see the most on, Guvner, is the Sreekin' [shrieking] Wumman what nearly always run about the hills arter twelve o' clock."

"But," said the listener, "have you really seen the lady, m' lad - or is it just tradition?"

The fisherman hesitated a bit, while the latter part of the sentence was juggled with; he eventually replied, "T'int no larfin matter a cos I ha' sin a, so ha' a lot more on us."

He went on, "We war all fishing along the beach one night - a linin' f'r cod when we hard terrible sreeks uvver in the walley.

When we look round we see har a runnin' athowt the hills sreekin' like hell. All the other fellers but me hulled [hurled] down thar gear an' run like med."

"So you were the brave boy of the crew - you stuck at your post." said the visitor.

"It worn't a'cos I wus brave," replied the man, "I wus too b------ frightened to run!"

UNFOUNDED!

[A sad story but all too common in the days of fishing from sailing ships[

The man who carted nets and gear for the local boat owners often brought, as well as fisherman's wages to their wives, clothes to be 'overhauled' and general news of the fishing sphere to the many interested in the village.

One day he had to communicate some bad news to one of the women -one who was an excellent housewife, but not too brilliant in other respects, however.

The following dialogue ensued:-

Carter "Now, Martha, I don't wantcha at teke things tu hard, but I 'a got some bad news at tell ya."

Martha "Oh Henera **[Henry]** don't yow come tryin' to frighten the life outa me, whataver ya du."

Carter "I wantcha at be ez brave ez ya ken, Martha, cus I heered your William 'a bin hulled overboard in a rough sea.

Martha: "Oh but I know my husbin int drowned, Henera - du he sent me a pus-card like he done afore when he wus lorst.

CONSEQUENCES

In this story George pays homage to Charles Dickens who clearly influenced him much. He is mocking the too faced standards of an older generation and again I suspect it is intended as a satire on residents of Hemsby known to Mr. Beech

In appearance and outlook the old lady bore a striking resemblance to the famous Dickensian character Sairey Gamp. **[The Gin Swilling Midwife in Martin Chuzzlewit]** There, however, the similarity ended - for as we have never read the illustrious Sairey had fifteen children of her own although she had introduced many to this suffering world. Well Mrs. Haricot had: moreover their respective fathers were missing - possibly 'drowned at sea, at an early age'.

Let the public assume in their back-door gossip what they like in regard to them - all we know is that the offspring were noisily in evidence.

This buxom old lady was entertaining her bosom friend to tea one day. Of course the conversation ran in the usual channel, mostly scandal - hence the following:-

Mrs. Geezer: I hare that young Dorotha Jackson a gotta youngster!"

Mrs. Haricot: "An she's unly seventeen, neither - I reckon things are comin' at suffin ammun' these mawthers round hare."

Mrs Geezer: "So they are tu, Jinny bor; I wonder what 'ud of happened at us if we'd a done like thet when we war gels?"

Mrs. Haricot: "Lawkes-a-massy, Hannah, we'd a hed our legs cut orf!"

THE MISSING POSTS

The following story I believe is based on an incident that took place where a local dishonest builder was caught out by the village policeman who came from London. I feel George's attempt at writing in 'Cockney' is a lot less successful than his Norfolk portrayals.

* * *

On our dunes is a strange assortment of hutments, usually let in the summer months. Socially one would be shocked to have one's structure termed 'hut', as the owners prefer to call them 'bungalows' although to a stranger with any artistic discernment, they would appear to be, mainly atrocious shacks.

From around one of these beach dwellings a supposed paled fence had been built and this had been carried away ostensibly for kindling.

The carpenter and the author of the imagined fence, having a further job in mind wrote to the owner telling him what was supposed to have occurred, asking if he should replace it.

Weeks elapsed and no order came.

One day as the tradesman was waiting to board the bus for Yareham, the local police-constable, a Londoner, approached him and said, "Ah Sid, you're just the man hi want to see."

"I can't stop now - I'm a gorn' to town; I'll have a yarn wi' yow another time." retorted Sid, off handedly.

P.C. "Never mind gowin' to tarn for a moment, Sid. Hi want to 'ear abart those posts that were pinched from from Mr. ------'s 'ut."

Sid: (resignedly) "Orl right then; should we go down an' hev a look round?"

P.C.: "Yes, Hi think so. Hi want ter tike a few nowts abart the cise."

They arrive at the scene of depredation.

P.C.: "So this is the 'ut - and the posts were all rahnd 'ere up to that 'edge there, hi suppowse ?"

Sid: "Ya thet's where they wor."

P.C.: (puzzled) "Well if the posts were hall rahnd the 'ut, dozens of 'em - where have the 'oles gorn?"

Sid: (fed up) "Oh, I reckon them b-------s tuk them an' all.

SOME POETRY BY G.W.B.

OUR ANCIENTS

Hemsby Church and Barn Room acted as "Church Rooms" and Meeting Hall for many years. It was modernised in 1972 and 2006 and has all facilities except for a seat for old men to watch the world go by.

Now, here's to our oldest inhabitants,
Old Billy, old Jack and old Sam,
They thrive on mild beer and tobacco.
And many a long mile they jam*.

There's a seat put in front of the 'Barn Room',
Where the octogenarians meet,
A seat where they sit in the sunshine,
And get a nice view of 'The Street'

So many a good yarn in the summer,
Is spun to the visitors oft-
Of smugglin' and feeshin' and pawking,**
Of 'wath'rin' the gaele up aloft.

Now, their Norfolk dialect , Reader,
To the stranger sounds it damn queer,
Still, they seem amused by the stories,
So they fill up the old 'uns with beer,

There's a saying among our old fishers-
"Who give ya' a pint is orl right
But when they heng on wi' out askin',
We call it a blasted Blue Light"

The dresses of our modern young women,
They laugh at, and treat with much scorn,
For when these lads went after the mawthers,***
The dear old crinoline was worn.

I've heard them, jokingly, tell the youngsters,
(With a touch of envy, I'll vow,)
"Yow c'n hold the young gels a lot closer,
Cus ya' hint no sich obstiggles now."

Glossary. for those unfamiliar with the Norfolk vocabulary.
* Jam = walk .**Pawking = beach combing.
***.Mawthers = girls.

Some of them tell you about old hosses;
Old masters they've had in their time;
A few of them can even remember,
Hearing all of our church bells chime.

Some can recall how all of our farmers,
Made most of their varied crops pay;
Just as others remember the time too,
When our pubs were open all day.

At Christmas, in those days, they've told us
The village was full of good cheer,
In the bars of the Bell and the King's Head,
The floors were waist-deep in good beer.

If one read' in their day, on a Sunday
One asked for a free pass to hell;
And parents put wind up the youngsters
By terrible ghost-yarns they'd tell.

Here's good health to Old Bob, and Old Billy,
Old Jack, Old Jerry and Old Fred;
You have had a hard time in your youth, Lads,
But now, you're a long way from dead

So, just keep up your stunt in the summer-
Smoke your 'Norton's Shag' and drink ale-
All that the young furriners will give you,
Whether a half-pint or a pail.

For, all of us do want you to hang on
As long as you can to this place,
You old sea-beaten natives we're proud of
The scions of East Norfolk's race.

As you sit on that seat near the Churchyard
You can gaze, and ponder a lot,
For, Old father Time stands by your elbow,
So just keep an eye on a plot.

Hemsby Church and Street circa 1925. The dog and the cyclist would not last long today although when reading the 12th December 1931 edition of the 'Yarmouth Mercury' I noted in the Yarmouth Mercury Hemsby Parish News 'Mr. Beech's retriever Rex was killed by a motor car near the Bell!'. Reporters were very thorough in those days.

EAST NORFOLK IDYLL

Girded by the waves that lash the golden sand,
And beat the tall sheer cliffs of clay
Which fringe the Hamlets on the Norfolk strand,
And keep the wild North Sea at bay.

The Hundred of the Flegg; a full two score,
Of tiny parishes that spring
From Dane and Norse at the core;
At Fleggburgh they held their Althing.

The winding lokes; plantations, grassy cotes;
The fields of golden corn in ear;
The whitewashed inns the longshore boats;
The dunes; the Broads - you have them here.

Now, mark the sun-kissed orchards by the way,
And note encircled village green
By quaint old pebble housen, Norfolk thatched;
Flint churches, ivy grown are seen.

The kindly fisher folk, the sun bronzed men
Who turn the furrow flete, nearby,
And strapping blue eyed mawthers of the fen
Shall for your interest, Reader vie.

OUR FISHERMEN

[This poem does not scan]

He's a fisher-lad bold,
Always cheery and free,
His work is damn hard,
His home's on the sea.

From Parents and sweetheart
Ashore ,he's gone forth
To catch the deep sea herring,
Far up in the North.

No matter it blows a gale,
And the wild billows race
To swamp the old Drifter-
There's a grin on his face.

He'll 'do his bit' always,
When afloat, or on land,
At hauling or stowing
The fleet of nets, tanned,

So, up with mizzen
And make Yarmouth Wharf;
May yours be top boat, yonker, **[Youngster]**
When the fleet is paid orf.

OUR SEXTON

[This poem is about Richard Gowan (Little Dick) noted for pronouncing 'vs.' as 'ws'.]

Kind friend, my life is werra hard,
Toilin' wiv pick an speared;(spade)
I grub all day in our charchya'd
A' coverin' up the dead.

Some would call har a nasty job,
But for thar's I don't sigh,
For, why in course, tha's how I live-
''Cus uvver beggers die.

An' arter all, I'm happy when,
I'm tollin our big bell.
For ,how ken thet affec' my narves-
Annuver feller's knell?

The Wicar allus come at me
When some one's teaken' orf,
An' show me where to plant 'em in,
I nod my hid an' corf.

For if they all lived to the age
Of Mefooslah, old an' hoary,
You ken krite see, thet I sh'd starve,
An' thet 'ud end my story.

When at the farnace, down I go,
And prug among the coals,
It make me fink of bad ole Nick,
A' roastin' poor damed souls,

I set in Charch a Sunday night,
A cold seat at the end,
I shiver, and try not at cough,
Tha' s hard at' say 'Ah-men',

An' when, kind friends , I'm nearla orf,
A' dozin' in my pew
The Sidesman smack me on the back
An' holler till he's blue.

For wiv them all' I git no rest,
From good-uns' or from bad'uns;
Thar all the searm, they wurra me-
'Specially when thar dead uns.

I git my own back later on,
An' chuckle when I rod 'em
An' jest afore I clean my speared
I look around - an sod 'em.

I believe the man with the bass drum is Richard Gowan Junior the village sexton. I have been told that Dick would dance on some coffins if he disliked the deceased but this could be apocryphal.

OUR BUTCHER'S DREAM

[This poem refers to a time when meat was produced in the Village and animals were slaughtered locally.]

Our Butcher once, when work was done,
And all the meat hung up to dry,
And all the chitterings boiled in milk,
And kidneys detached from the fry
Betook him home.

He sat him down, at board he ate
Of pork and apple pie divine
To him after slogging all the day,
And finished with some rare old wine
From out the store.

He pulled his lounge chair to the fire,
And from the logs a cheroot he lit;
With brimming tankard right at hand,
He got cash-book to balance it '
And see his gain

Now as he smoked and drank his wine
And gazed at row on row of numbers
The columns seem to merge together,
And soon our Butcher was a'slumber
Afore the fire.

He lay as comfy as could be;
His burnt cheroot fell from the holder;
And as he sprawled upon his chair,
He felt a tap upon his shoulder
That wakened him.

He looked with wide amazed eyes
The demmed intruder to behold,
But at the sight confronted him
Our Butcher turned as mutton cold
And all a'shake.

For gaunt, and standin by his side
Was a bullock, wild, and steeped in gore,
And pigs, that numbered seven, quite ,
Were gathered , bloody by the door,
All on tip-toes.

A sheep had coiled, upon his hoof
A hempen cord, the noose was dangling;
The bullock said, "It's your turn now,
So get a move on without wrangling;
Your numbers up."

"For forty years you've kidded us,"
The bullock said, "Afore the kill
With your sweet tongue and sweeter hay;
We've got you now, and so we will
To pay you out."

They roped our Butcher fast and tight,
And led him forth from out his room,
Through the yards that reeked of blood
Into a cold night, cast with gloom
He shivered so.

At last he found himself inside
The charnel house he knew so well;
The pigs danced round him all the time-
They were like fiends escaped from hell,
With gleaming eyes.

The windlass they had got to work,
And strain'd and tauten'd was the noose
Around his neck the sheep had placed
For fear our Butcher should get loose,
And flee off hand.

In vain he cried, " For pity's sake!"
In vain he struggled for his life;
The Bullock stood with gleaming eye,
Clove hoof 'a grasping fast , a knife
So deadly sharp.

The hellions screaming danced with glee
T'was last he saw, the knife went home;
Our Butcher knew his hour had come;
The dim light threw their shadows round;
His life-blood fled.

One piecing scream the old man gave
That shook the walls, ere all was o'er-
(Poor chap he'd just slipped from his chair,
His wife then raised him from the floor,)
His dream was done.

Now please, you gourmands, hearken here,
At night when you sit down to dine-
If you've a pork and apple pie-
Don't make the 'night-cap' rare old wine
Else dream you will.

The Butcher's Shop is on Pit Road The building beyond this, now a cake shop which used to be the slaughter-house. The Spar Shop beyond that was the school before it was burned down at beginning of the last century. It was demolished in 2005 and replaced by houses.(Photograph A. J. Fakes c 1980)

OUR BRICKLAYERS

This poem refers to my family among others. George refers to FXXXXs trio which I believe refers to my Grandfather's business A. J. Fakes Builders being Arthur Johnson Fakes. Wiggy refers to my father, Arthur Charles Fakes, who gained this nick-name not because of any hair piece but as a child he pronounced his elder brother William or Willy's name as Wiggy. The name became transferred to my father to distinguish him from his father also Arthur.
(Note the italics refer to building trade terms)

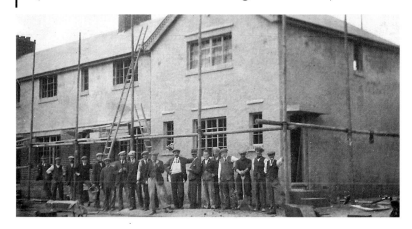

Building Council House between the Wars by A.J. Fakes in Station Road Ormesby.

You'll find them here, in *Proper Bond,*
Our brickies, jocular and gay,
They *Head The Courses,* of their lives
By working well each blessed day.

There's Jumbo veteran of the *Trowel,*
For ages he's been *on the Line,*
He dresses still in tradesmans *Cords,*
And smokes, unceasing, his 'Woodbine'.

Go seek ye round in Cot or Hall,
There's not a job he cannot do
To *Copper, Register or Range;*
He specializes on each *Flue.*

We'll take the Fxxxxs trio next-
To Arthur, Bert and Wiggy come;
Though at times their *joints are Loose,*
You'll never find 'em *Out Of Plumb.*

Now Georgie Fxxx and Freddy Rxxx,
We mustn't *Snub* tho' strangers here;
'Tis said the *Lime* gets in their throats,
And they must *Slake* their thirsts in beer.

Two Kings called Fred are working here;
As to their crimes I'll say I'm baffled-
But, hardened sinners they must be-
For, every day they mount the *Scaffold.*

There's Ashley Hxxx, a *Level* fellow;
Sometimes, a *Stretcher;* always *Square;*
He'll pull your leg, at times dryly,
On Ashley's *Face* a smile is rare.

All these good *Old English* workmen
Will *Drift* along when toil is o'er.
And *Jamb* to Ale-House on the corner,
To call for pints they've sweated for.

See their jovial faces *Crimson,*
The *Camber* of their noses glow,
As each a brimming *hod* he empties'
And adds his quota to the *Row.*

The-morning-after-night-before
Breaks on our pals, they leave their *Bed,*
Their feet can hardly feel the *Pavements,*
They seem to have a *Concrete Head.*

Now as a *Closer ,* I'll remark,
As *Roofs* are raised and *Poles* are struck,
I wish them *Quoins* to come in plenty;
Their *Finials* always be 'Good Luck'.

For, in our work they form the *Centre;*
The *Keystone* of the Building Trade;
Their good work will outlast the time
When in the *Trench* themselves are *laid.*

When, down below, they get a get a *Footing,*
Where *leading hand* is Bad Old Nick,
An endless job they'll have before them,
A 'lining Hxxx with *fire brick.*

Until then old friends don't worry'
Just *Raise Your Corner* with good cheer;
Cement comradeship with your chummies
With Steward and Patterson's famous beer.

Jumbo on the right with Woodbine. (Mrs S Smith).

Jumbo refers to Jumbo Woodhouse who was typical of many workers on building sites in that he has able to state great truths and general wisdom very briefly but usually in coarse terms. Jumbo's Law of Economics was "You can't pull out a bigger one than what you got!"

My father used to tell the tale of Jumbo and a man who I shall call Mr. X. He was from a well-to-do family but was an incurable alcoholic (and to Jumbo's disgust was in denial). If he had money he would drink himself senseless. Jumbo was not feeling very tolerant on a building site when he said to my father "Here comes b***** old X drunk as muck as usual". Mr. X remarked, "Why, Mr. Woodhouse you've never seen me inebriated." Jumbo's reply was "I've seen you p***** plenty of times. What about last week when I saw you crawling about on your hands and knees in Somerton" Mr. X said "Ah Mr. Woodhouse I was knocked down by a lorry." Jumbo never lost for words said "That must have been a Lacon's Lorry" (Lacon's being the local brewery)

Mr. X's family partially solved the problem by not letting him have any cash but paying for a daily pint of beer at about five pubs in the district and Mr. X had to walk between each pub before he could get a drink. This system was used for similar cases and the people were referred to as a 'Remittance Men.'

OUR OLD TUTOR

Richard Cobden Jones the Headmaster of Hemsby School for many years is on the extreme right. George clearly held him in some respect and affection. The teacher on the left became my aunt Ruby Fakes nee Boate. My father was not happy when his teacher started to 'walk out' with his eldest brother

From Cambria, mountainous and wild,
Full three-score years ago, and more
A Master came to our new school-
A stranger to this Norfolk Shore.

Our people, sturdy Eastern breed,
So insular; conservative;
They at our Welshman looked askance
At first, when he came here to live

They thought from scanty History learne'd
In far off days, and seemed to hit on
Thro' rustic logic, he from Wales
Must be, of course, an Early Briton!

Instead of clerical dress arrayed
A tiger skin should drape his frame;
In lieu of evening-dress he should
Apply some woad- 't were all the same.

The years went on, our pedagogue,
More understood, and understanding
His rural neighbours, cold and dour,
Their dialect; their clannish banding.

Day after day, and year by year,
The hardest job that one could do
He had; infusing Norfolk Youth-
That job would turn most masters 'blue'.

The same old round- no 'trivial task',
The curriculum each day he taught,
And gave his well-earned leisure hours
To public work - he said was naught.

Then came The War, that great upheaval;
He saw his erstwhile scholars wend
Into that vortex --- merely lads;
Why hide that tear --- O mentor ---friend?

He plodded on his school life,
An uphill task, and thankless quite;
His joie de vivre left him not.
But, aged now, his hair is white.

He's seen his son, grandchildren too,
From childhood grow, and sally forth
Into a mundane business life,
And settle far up in the North.

'Near yonder copse' - a garden smiles;
His duties o'er here's his retreat;
No crowd of eager faces there;
No board easel; classroom neat.

Here in the autumn of their lives,
Our Master and our Governess dwell
Alone, in well-deserved seclusion;
Their cottage in flower bordered dell.

He has his poultry and his bees;
His horticultural vocation;
With wireless and book-shelf stocked,
Its versatile - his occupation.

Generations of village Youth,
Back to the schooldays gone, will hark;
Recall the sprees, when under JONES-
Their Master: helper 'Anwyl bach'.

Note by G.W.B.
I much regret to announce that since these lines were written "Our Old Tutor" Richard Cobden Jones has passed into the Great Beyond.
A friend to all, the community has sustained a great loss by his passing.
"Vivat post funera virtus"

During his school days my father always referred to Mr. Jones as RC but he learned to quote tracts of poetry for the rest of his life. He was particularly fond of 'How Horatius Kept the Bridge in the Brave Days of Yore' and 'The Burial of Sir John More at Corruna.'

OUR SMITHY

There's a pretty little Smithy down the loke,
You can see it by its cloud of chimney-smoke,
Our blacksmiths gailey sing,
Jack Thurtle and Boss King.
As they draw the red hot irons from the coke.

Now, our Smithy is as old as many hill,
Is being built in the youth of old King Will;
It has 'seen the times' indeed,
And every class of steed
From the donkey to the motor-tractor drill.

Here are wheels for e'vry vehicle that's seen
Some are orange, others sky-blue many green
There are wheels for the tram,
The milk float and the pram,
From the scooter, tumbrel and the limousine.

When they were short of shrapnel in the war
The Government sent a note to King for more
Old bedsteads shoes and nails,
Old plough-shares, tyres and pails,
He sent them off to Woolwich by the score.

From dawn of day the noisy bellows roar,
There's a queue of horses by the open door,
For Jack will peg away
At striking shoes all day,
While his master, with the callers do the jaw.

For, the Smithy is the general house of call,
Our blacksmith loves to chat to one and all
Of hosses and the crops
Of the Gov'ment, but stops
When some clever jokes on him begin to fall.

Around the forge, the sparks, in showers fly,
And you must be dam careful standing by.
They hammer with a zest,
And never want to rest
'Til the missis calls that 'fourses-time' is nigh.

Always, at a certain season of the year
The Master Blacksmith generates good cheer,
He asks him to drink-
You'll hear their glasses clink-
For, between 'em is a cask of Ginger-Beer.

There is one thing our old smith hasn't got;
It's a thing he would appreciate a lot;
He'd be pleased as could be
If he'd a chestnut-tree;
So, will someone send a cutting in a pot?

For, exactly like the blacksmith in the song
Although he's got rather ancient, he is strong,
So ere our friend is dead
Let him see a chestnut spread
Then hasten someone ; send the gift along.

Let us trust that modern craze for speed
Will not find the horses, tractors supercede;
We want our forge a' glowing
And still hear bellows blowing,
And have our honest Smith supply the need.

OUR PUBLIC MEETING

[Parish politics don't alter much between generations.]

Hearken all ye nobles of our Village
Ye bourgoise, ye rural girls and boys-
The Elders met in state t'other evening
On the vexed question of combating noise.

It appears in summer months , the Campers
After squatting many months on office stool
Bottling up their mirth, their witty chatter
Release it here at night - and play the fool.

Now, let it not be believed that we grudge
Such hard -won frolic due to this young flock ,
But citizens are apt to get ferocious
If wakened from their rest at one o'clock

Brother Bxxxx got heated in debating -
Said he heard 'em at the midnight, on the ramp,
And the naughty ballad they were singing
Had shocked his finer feelings
                    "Shut the Camp!"

Said this incensed burgher, "At eleven-
Or let the parish Cop put them in the clink-
I don't go a' agriwatin' people,
Even when I' hed my little drink,"
                    "Shut the Camp!"

Eastern Members on their feet-
"Pooh ! Pooh! My dear sir I might say as well,
Close down that Emporium of hardware,
Grocery, Sausages -near the Bluebell!."

During the discussion a Patriach said,
"Although in this I'm in no way a prude,
I heartily wish to see something done
As I've heard they often bathe in the nude."

"When Adam lived here in those olden times,
He and Eve, frolicsome, dipped in the sea,
As neighbours were few, it worried them not'
To get bathing dress from a handy fig tree,

"But now," quoth he, "We civilized are,
Though the Crinoline seems de-trop today-
Its hard that my pure minded breatheren have
To meet fair damsels dressed so *negligee,*

For Mrs. Grundy lives among us still,
Her mittened hands she raises in alarm;
She says "Our Youth is dreadfully immoral!
But most of us will answer "Merely warm."

This public meeting in Hemsby was held in 1981 to decide on a memorial to for Mr. Beech. It was not contentious but only enough money was raised to pay for a seat outside the new Doctor's Surgery.

For as Laurence Sterne said in his time-
"Prudes rather *envy*, than abhor the crime!"

An item came up in the agenda,
The angry village blocked it might and main,
For, what with sewers, gulleys and pipe-lines
It seemed that some had 'water' on the brain.

Ever since the Flood our little Parish
Has drawn its water quota from the well,
For ablution mostly, through clean and clear;
The thirsty peon quenched it at the 'Bell',

Certain lazy settlers here would have us
Exchange for urban tap the rural tub,
Drink and wash in water from the river-
The river with a aggregate of slub.

Had they passed it, what a fine old muddle-
We'd have the plumber with his mate to train
Fixing cocks and waste-traps to the hip-bath,
And every cottage privy have its chain.

The outcome of all this twaddle and talk,
The arguments vague, the bunkum and rot-
A commision be formed to report on't,
Record of which would be shelved and forgot.

91

OUR POLICEMAN

Fred Lister (Centre) looking very stern and serious. He was village constable from well before the Second World War. On his retirement from after the war he became Landlord of the King's Head. I remember many of the Policemen based in Hemsby as quite 'hard' men as they could only rely on themselves unlike today when help and reinforcements can be summoned by radio and arrive by car in minutes. P.C Herber(Joe) Reeves followed Fred. He was followed by Gordon Juby, then Derek Elliot, who all three became sergeants Then Herbert (Pete) Parsley and finally Chris Pointer was the last 'Village' Policeman in Hemsby. The concept of Parish Constable has been replaced by Community Policing.

Our Policeman's life is hard, in deed,
On his large country beat.
Plodding over miles of tarmac
With number fifteen feet.

You'll find him patrolling our Street
Good natured, tall and well,
Guiding tactfully the traffic
A 'surging round 'The Bell'

He will always do his duty
And watch the bare legged throng,
For he'll soon haul out his note-book
If frocks are none too long.

For, some of the pretty camp-girls
On holiday, so free,
Care nothing if their costume ends
A foot above the knee.

It makes our Copper embarrassed,
He shakes and turns quite white
When taking names of the culprits
By glimmer of his light.

Now, if a bold, bad burglar tried
To steal all Jack Smith's beer,
Or tamper with the Poor Box-
Is our guardian there?

No! perhaps he's on the marrams,
A' creeping with his torch
Around the little bungalows-
Watching out for debauch.

Or possibly, he is dozing
Under a straw-stack, warm;
Wherever he is, remember,
Its miles away from harm.

Still, our Policeman's always sporty,
In civvies or in blue;
Without the law he is human
At heart, like all of you.

So give our Cop an easy time,
Just keep away from sin,
For, if you pull old D.O.R.A's. leg,
He'll surely run you in.

I believe the name D.O.R.A. has a double meaning. Mrs. Lister's name was Dora and that the initials refer to the Defence of the Realm Act which over rode normal law in war time.

THE DUMPLING

The final chapter of George Beech's book 'Norfolk Medley' of 1941 is entitled "Local Customs"
It would have perhaps been better to call it 'In Praise of the Norfolk Dumpling'

Heaven forbid that we should conclude these Norfolk notes without a word about that well-known and exclusive dish - the Dumpling or to be exact, "Norfolk Swimmer"

I understand that our East Anglian brothers in Suffolk thrive on such a dumpling, called a "Suffolk Whelp" - the difference being, not in its components, but in its size; while we call a 20 minute dumpling the latter is termed a "half hour" ditto, these being the requisite periods they take to cook.

I am no chef-de-cuisine but I believe that Dumplings should be steamed rather than boiled. Boiling tends to make them an excellent substitute for high-grade leather.

In an era of large families with relatively enormous appetites, the ladies usually cooked their 'swimmers' by the copper-full a'top of the greens.

Far be it from me think that it cannot be done, but up to the present I have never been lucky in finding a 'furrin' housewife who could make success of cooking the Norfolk Dumpling, although many of them can serve up marvelous dishes of a much more intricate nature. The very simplicity of the Dumpling, which is but composed of flour salt and baking-powder seems to have beaten the ladies as they variously believe it to contain eggs, suet, tapioca, mincemeat or some ingredient foreign to it.

I have been promised as guest of honour in several strangers' houses 'A real Norfolk Dumpling' but on seeing the unholy, soggy mess masquerading under that name, knife and fork have fallen from my nerveless fingers and I have pushed away.

It may be advisable say at this juncture that the original dumpling makers used for a rising medium - yeast , preferably Brewer's Yeast.

Lack of this essential may account for the modern dumpling being a trifle 'heavy'.

I have never found their historical origin ; undoubtedly there are detractors of our county , who, in their profound knowledge, will readily tell us that these delicatessen were introduced into Norfolk by the Netherlanders, Danes or, possibly Lombards, but be this true or not - one thing is sure - they were adopted by thrifty and harassed housewives , as a filling when they had to rear large families on never more than ten shillings a week, and little more could be afforded.

Now, Reader, I will leave you to conjure up the vision of a Norfolk Swimmer swimming its lake of brown gravy. If your wife and or mother is also good at conjuring, cajole or bully her into providing the above dish - neither of you will regret it.

[The above were the final words written on page 74 of Norfolk Medley.]

> I feel that George Beech's writings should end with the Funeral Oration quoted in the Hemsby Parish News of November 1979 which though not stated I believe was spoken by Mr. William Lodder of Frostenden in Suffolk. He was the owner of 'Homestalls'. He was therefore George's landlord. I also feel that poem at the end is George's best in its simplicity and self mocking.

"I feel privileged to have been asked by the vicar to say a few words about George Beech as my wife and I count ourselves among his oldest friends.

We mourn today the passing of a remarkable man. George was born in Hemsby in 1901, in Homestalls in Pit Road, which was his home for the whole of his life. We have lost a friend but the village has lost an institution.

George's father and grandfather were master builders and it was assumed that George would follow their trade. He did in fact enter the business, but, after a few years, he decided to become a printer and embarked on the training for this with enthusiasm. Part of the training entailed the cutting of wooden type-faces for large letters, and it was this skill which led him into woodcarving. He set up 'The Flegg Press' which became an active business. At the same time he interested himself in carving oak and it was in this field that he is probably best known.

He preferred to make furniture in the style of the 17th century and pieces have gone to homes all over the country and abroad. You have, no doubt, seen many examples. In this church he assisted many years ago in the rebuilding of the roof and made the gates.

He was an excellent sign writer, using his wide knowledge of type-faces, and his house name boards are to be found throughout the village. What is not so well known, however, was his literary tastes and abilities. He read widely, he taught himself Latin, French and some German. He loved Dutch and Danish history, and in particular to debate the rights and wrongs of historical events with anyone who would argue with him. His knowledge of the works of Dickens was stupendous, and his impressions of some of the characters were most entertaining. It was inevitable that he should want to write and in a little volume, written in 1941, he fulfilled his ambition to emulate Caxton; to write something, print it and bind it. This he did and adopted the pen-name Rusticus a countryman.

We are fortunate that he decided to record his 'History of Hemsby'. Life was not easy for George. The depression of the 1930s hit his family hard. He never married, but to his intimate friends, he spoke of a girl he loved in his youth. He nursed his mother and father with great care and under difficulties in the late 1950s. He asked that he should be buried near them and his grandparents in the Congregational Churchyard. He was a man of great integrity. He stood by his word and his promise was sacred. He was fiercely independent and never retired from work.

This verse was written by George many years ago. It is entitled in the Latin 'Vale'. It means 'Farewell'.

When falls the night on me, a unit,
Of this vast organization, life;
When I dream the dream that ends not,
Away from cares and useless strife.
Try friend to erase from your memory,
The faults, the follies you knew me do,
And think that through the years,
That I've been sincere to you.
And when my voice is but a whisper,
That echoes down the halls of time.
Recall that Norfolk friend of yours,
Who wrote his thoughts for you in rhyme."

"Rusticus" George William Beech 1901 -1979.

Hemsby Congregational Church is on Yarmouth Road. Near the path lies the remains of Albert Adrian Beech, his wife Jane and their son George William Beech. To date they do not have a memorial in the grave yard which I feel is a shame not least because I am inveterate reader of gravestones but I feel that Hemsby should commemorate one of its most notable sons.
A. J. Fakes, November 2010.

THE SECOND WORLD WAR IN HEMSBY

George Beech lived through the Second World War but chose not to describe his feelings in any depth as it did not give him many memories that he felt he should record. Indeed he gives more details of the more costly struggle he would have called the Great War. Hemsby lost 20 men in the just over four years of WW1 and lost a further eight in the near six years World War Two.

I was asked by someone at Hemsby School in 2007 what happened in the Second World War in the village. I wrote two pages of my thoughts. I then spoke to people who had experience of the war years. By the very nature of things I was only able to speak to people who were young at the time some sixty years earlier. These people gave a positive view as I suspect they were too young to appreciate the possible danger they were in.

However, I recall a conversation with my mother about 40 years ago in which she described her situation in 1940. She said "Your father was called up into the army. Your brother was a very young baby. There were only women, children and old men in the village. Food was short. We were ordered to pack one suitcase in case we had to be evacuated if we had been invaded." She then went on to make the most obvious remark which I confess I had not considered until that point."Of course we didn't know who was going to win the war then." My mother had good reason to fear war because her father, Robert Prentice, a Norwich plumber was in the army in France during the First War where he survived a gas attack but died in his early forties of respiratory problems.

Inevitably there was anti-German feeling carried forward from the previous war which had cost Britain dear in money and lives. The citizens of Hemsby had little direct experience of Germans as ordinary people. The attitude was 'We beat the Huns in the last war and we'll beat them again.' Peter Matthews recalls November 5th in 1938 when an effigy of Hitler was burned instead of Guy Fawkes.

David Cook who lived with his family in Newport Cottages told me he recalled his Grandfather reading the paper to him before the war when he was six or seven. He was very frightened by the possibility of being bombed with gas or high explosives and what war would bring. When the actual war came David was fascinated by what the soldiers were doing in building 'Pill Boxes', concrete tank traps, scaffold fences and laying mines. He said the soldiers were friendly and talked with the children. David went on to scar his hand by hitting some of the bullets he had found with a hammer!

Fear of a German attack, particularly after Dunkirk ensured that the East Coast of England would be heavily defended in 1940. As many as three pill boxes were built at Newport one being disguised as a wooden bungalow. Some buildings on the sand hills were removed to give the guns 'a clear line of sight. A

Hemsby Gap circa 1950 the concrete blocks across the gap can be clearly seen as can the pill box but they are being covered by sand. Note also the Radar Tower at Winterton (Mr. Russell Smith's Collection)

double row of concrete blocks were laid across Hemsby Gap with a further pill box on the beach. Anti boat scaffolding was erected on the beach and mines were laid on the sand hills.

The blocks in the Gap were built by men of the Royal Engineers and the Pioneer Corps under Sergeant Tom Hanbury from Pontypool in Wales who remained in Hemsby as a plumber and engineer after the War.

Further pill boxes were built on King's Loke facing the fields towards Winterton, on Beach Road by the entrance to Maddieson's Camp, on the railway line behind that camp, on the corner opposite the Post Office to control the crossroads and on the junction of North Road and Waters Lane to control the road to Martham. In spite of all this effort it was felt that the Wermact would have only been briefly slowed down by these obstacles as they would have gone round them in their 'Panzers'. In the Polish Campaign the Germans surrounded pill boxes with smoke and attacked them from short range with flame throwers. The Home Guard felt less vulnerable in open country which they knew well rather than in pill boxes with a limited angle of fire. The programme of building pill boxes stopped in 1942

Left. The Pill Box by the Railway Line proved too difficult to knock down so it was buried under a mound and Pontins placed their hoarding on it. Middle: shows Pill Box on King's Loke facing the fields towards Winterton. A Pill Box stood in Mr. Clemmy Church's garden to command the crossroads opposite the Post Office but was quickly removed. I assume this was not one of the more solid concrete structures.

A force of L.D.Vs. (Local Defence Volunteers) was recruited in Hemsby which became the Home Guard. Harry Maddieson who owned the Holiday Camp was Captain with Mr. Fred Chinnery the Station Master as Lieutenant.

I'm told that a German plane was seen from Newport early in the war it was there for sometime 'droning up and down'. It was not challenged. Shortly afterwards a collier and a trawler were blown up off Caister by magnetic mines. There was only one survivor.

In the summer of 1940, the Battle of Britain would have been clearly in evidence over Hemsby with a great number of enemy aircraft overhead but, famously, the R.A.F. eventually got the better of the Luftwaffe.

Around this time a dinghy was seen floating off Newport and the soldiers building the defences persuaded Herbert (Brusher) Hall to row his boat out to pick up the occupants. He was accompanied by a sergeant with a rifle. There were four German airmen in the dinghy. They panicked because they thought they were going to be abandoned at sea when Brusher rowed past them. However, what was happening Mr. Hall's seamanship dictated he should pull the men in over the stern of his boat which was the place least likely to tip it up. The airmen told their rescuers that they had been shot over the Channel and had crash landed in the North Sea. My informant told me of an ungallant act by a British Soldier, called Ginger, who made a fire to brew tea for the rescued party. On learning they were German he kicked the fire out.

I was also told of an incident at the Holiday Camp when German airmen were brought in and a soldier suggested they should be shot for what they had been doing. Wiser councils prevailed and the Geneva Conventions were observed and they were not shot. However, there was strong feeling against the enemy which had killed women and children.

HOW PEOPLE SAW THE WAR

The perception of war would have been gained from newspapers and the radio and cinema news-reels which were controlled by Government but people saw and heard things and they talked to each other. Ships were sunk and there was a great number of German aircraft over this country during the Battle of Britain. The number of allied aircraft in the sky would have been very noticeable. Up to one thousand bombers would assemble over the east coast of England, the U.S.A.A.F. by day and the R.A.F by night, to bomb Nazi occupied Europe only stopping for bad weather. During the latter part of the war German bombing tactics were limited to fast hit and run bombing which was inaccurate but could be lethal. Fortunately these became infrequent after the middle of 1943.

People in Hemsby would have been aware of a bomb which dropped on Martham on 4th September1940 which killed a 12 year old girl. Two women were killed by German bombing in Winterton on 7th May 1943. Several cottages were also destroyed during this raid and on 11th May 1943 a woman was killed in Ormesby by a bullet fired from a German aircraft. Also Great Yarmouth was heavily bombed throughout the war.

People would have heard of members of the armed forces being killed or wounded in action and of people reported as missing or captured by enemy forces.

Mr. Harold Tennant told me that he was shot at by a German aircraft early in the war. He was driving a horse and cart on the road at Dow Hill as a boy. Some bullets went in front of him and some passed behind him. He was not frightened at the time because he didn't know what was happening. Harold was living at Thornton Villa on North Road on 19th March 1943 when a parachute was seen floating down. Harold's father known as 'Pal' was in the Home Guard got his rifle hoping to arrest a German Airman or Spy. Unfortunately the parachute held a land mine (a bomb designed to explode above the ground and do damage over a wide area). The front door of Thornton Villa was blown all the way out of the back door into the garden Harold Senior reckoned he would have been killed if he had been in his hallway at the time. 50 properties were damaged by the raid on that day. Harold Junior recounts the most frightening part was controlling the terrified horses from their damaged stables to take to Mr. Jack King's farm who had agreed to accommodate them.

Geoff Smith recalls the sites where two bombs fell. One was on the east side of Winterton Road but it blew the front of a house on the west side where the Miss Spinneys lived. They were retired school teachers. The other fell in Nott's Plantation near Hall Farm. It made a crater which became a pond until it was filled in.

M. Derek Groom recounted an incident when the village policeman seemed to appear from nowhere as a German aeroplane flew over head. It was felt that a man, who was a 'Conscientious Objector' to military service, was an enemy spy. It was thought he was signaling in Morse by torch to a German Pilot of suitable targets to bomb. This, of course, was not true but it illustrates the state of fear and even paranoia which existed at that time.

Audrey McDermott nee Cook told me of an unfortunate incident which happened near her cottage at Newport during the war. The sand hills were fenced off because they were mined but a dog got into the minefield. It triggered an explosion. She returned to her home to brush herself down but when she combed her hair a piece of dog fell out

Audrey and her brothers lived with their parents in Newport Cottages throughout the war. Their house was shot at by gun fire from an aeroplane. They 'flew' down stairs where their mother pulled them under the table and the family was fortunately uninjured. The house next door had its bedroom hit by bullets but its usual occupant was fire watching. Audrey recalled finding a cannon shell on her dressing table.

Their father, Mr. George Cook was on his way to work at Neave's of Catfield where he built boats and pontoons. He saw the same raid unaware of the danger at his own house. He said that a Focke Wulfe 190 dropped a bomb near Hemsby Railway Station which bounced and exploded harmlessly in Mr. Tyson's field on Newport Road but he noted the plane banked and lost height. It hit an electricity pole and he assumed it had crashed.

Newport Cottages c1950. Their chimneys and roofs were damaged by German Cannon Fire 7/5 1943

David Cook said "It all seemed to happen in a split second then everything went quiet. We came out of the house, we found Mrs. Louie Cox covered in muck repeating 'I'm on fire! I'm on fire! She was not on fire but the bullets hitting her chimney had brought down her reed ceiling releasing the dust and muck of ages. I looked out to sea and saw the tail of an aeroplane sticking out of the water with an oil-slick drifting towards Yarmouth The body of the pilot washed ashore and was carried from the beach by Robert Turner and three others two days later"

Audrey recalls seeing the body covered by a blanket but there were two feet sticking out indicating that the man must have been tall. The pilot's papers gave his name as Willi Freudenriech aged 28. He was buried at Caister Cemetery on May 1943 but his body was moved to the Cemetery at Cannock Chase in the 1960s.

I was told of another lucky escape by an employee of Neave's of Catfield. Cyril Gibbs was walking along by the railway line where the Barleycroft estate now stands. A German plane dropped a bomb in the gardens on The Avenue. The bomb bounced and exploded in an empty field but the blast blew Cyril over the railway line leaving him only slightly injured but his lunch bag was found caught at the top of a telegraph pole!

Mr. Bernard Bould of Martham told me of an incident which happened to his uncle Mr. Victor Locke of Rollesby who worked with his brother for Charlie Wharton. They were ploughing with a tractor in the field beside the railway line at Martham Road Hemsby when Victor saw his brother leap off the tractor and dash to the ditch. Victor laughed as he thought his brother must have been 'taken very short' but then he noticed a bullet from an aeroplane had just gone past his head. On looking at his cap he found scorch marks from the bullet. This cap remained in his house for many years

Mr. Harold Church told me that he volunteered to join the Local Defence Volunteers which soon became the Home Guard. Mr. Church said that, possibly because Hemsby was on the coast, the company was issued with rifles from the start. There was no mention of pikes or broom sticks. The detail would assemble in the waiting room of Hemsby Railway Station and patrol the village at night in pairs on four hour watches. They were particularly looking out for parachutists and saboteurs. The volunteers not on duty would attempt to sleep on the wooden benches in the station. Mr. Church said he took part in one major exercise before he joined the Royal Air Force. He became a navigator flying Lancaster Bombers. He was shot down over Düsseldorf on 3rd November 1943 being one of the three who survived. He was detained in a Prisoner of War camp near the Polish border 'where several of us dug a tunnel in an attempt to escape but the unsporting Germans knew of this but allowed us to dig for weeks before descending upon us!' The camp was liberated by the Russians on 23rd April 1945 and he returned home in June.

CIVILIANS'S EXPERIENCE OF THE SECOND WORLD WAR

There were shortages of imported products and raw materials so ships brought only goods that were thought necessary for the war effort leaving almost everything in short supply. Most items were on ration but it was possible to obtain things on the 'black market' by paying above the proper price. Some people made fortunes in this way but it could lead to prosecution and simmering resentment from those unable to pay high prices. There seems to have been a great deal of barter in Hemsby whereby goods and services were exchanged thus not coming to the attention of the various Ministries and Food Controllers.

Farming had been neglected between the wars and many farmers, who were growing perfectly good crops, went bankrupt as they could only get poor prices for their harvest. When war came, farming was heavily regulated and a great deal of land, previously neglected was ploughed. Almost everything grown was used and farmers then began to receive a good income. As agricultural work was a 'Reserved Occupation', land workers could be exempt from being 'called-up' for military service.

John Green told me about a man who worked a small holding in Little Ormesby with his father but they had a lorry with a paraffin tank on it. They would go round the villages selling paraffin to various households. The young man described himself as a 'Paraffin Salesman' and was called up for military service. Had he claimed the less glamorous profession of 'Agricultural Labourer' he would have been exempt.

In the November 23rd November 1940 edition of the Yarmouth Mercury under 'News from the Villages' the following notes came from the Hemsby correspondent:- 11824 lb. of jam were made and sold at the 'Preserving Centre, all from fruit which would have been wasted. The Centre also sent 9½ tons of apples to a cider firm. I believe the Preserving Centre was at Hill House, the residence of Miss Jane Rudd. I also note she was later prosecuted for failing to fully close her curtains breaking the 'Black-Out' regulations. She told the court the maid was at fault.

Gathering wild fruit and 'gleaning' in the fields took on a new momentum. Catching rabbits, pigeons etc. for food became popular and profitable. Domestic refrigerators were almost unknown so much of the fruit and vegetables were preserved in sealed glass jars. Generally speaking the British People were healthier during the war than they had been previously or since. Rationing ensured a fair distribution of the food available. Less fatty and sweet food prevented obesity and tooth decay. Lack of motor transport made people take more exercise. One of George Beech's more notable comments on the subject was "Tha's that free Wartime Orange Juice made you children grow so tall!"

John Green told me of a further incident in May 1943 indicating agricultural work could be dangerous. Some farm workers were machine gunned in a field on Winterton Road, Hemsby and 'Rolly' Edmunds was shot through the leg and was bleeding heavily. John was on leave from the army at the time and in uniform. He took out a field dressing and staunched the blood flow. Dr. Paddy Rotchford was called and he administered morphine to the patient. 'Paddy wrote on Rolly's forehead with an 'indelible' pen the dose he had administered and he was taken to hospital.' However, on returning to barracks, John was asked to account for the missing dressing and told of the events that led to its use. The bad tempered officers of the Coldstream Guards said the cost would be deducted from John's wages.

I have heard it said often that the common adversity of the War made Hemsby a friendlier more united community, which, I'm sure is true to some extent.

The great changes the war made to civilian life in the area as a result of the movement of men and women for fighting the war were very noticeable. This brought excitement to the 'social life' of the district as well as the danger. Units of the Newfoundland Artillery were billeted into area early in the war and they seemed to have caused a flutter in the hearts of local maidens apparently to the annoyance of the local young men.

I quote from Mrs. Helen Gallaway's book 'Norfolk Dumplings' with her permission. Helen was born in Ormesby where her father Mr. John Freeman kept a shop.

"Summer came early that year, 1940, May was hot and sunny and a momentous month. My brother was called up and I was lonely. Village life seemed humdrum and small. Then one evening I got off the bus as usual (she was working at Boots the Chemists in Yarmouth then) and found the army had arrived to shatter the peace! Motor Bikes, armoured cars, lorries and Bren gun carriers occupied our roads and soldiers occupied the Manor and the Hall. What excitement for a quiet village! In our narrow lanes we'd never seen such activity, so many soldiers; in fact we'd never seen any real soldiers for we were un-travelled and had no television to enlighten us. The new Church Hall took on a different character and became very busy. Some evenings it turned into a canteen and we helped serve tea and buns. Other evenings, dances were held. The smell of hot khaki uniforms mingled with dust and French chalk from the floor, together with scents of the day 'Soir de Paris' and 'Californian Poppy'. We danced and danced to all the tunes of the day, and how romantic they were. Everybody danced and everybody knew all the songs and words. Victor Sylvester records supplied the music. This was excitement we thought and life with a capital L."

Mrs. Gallaway was the sister of John Freeman who lived in Hemsby for many years. She went on to become a Red Cross V.A.D. nurse in North Norfolk at Cranmer Hall Convalescent Home for the Forces. This was one of the many large houses taken over by Forces for this purpose. She wrote the following remarks for me as retrospective thoughts on the war.

"The War changed our lives completely - it was dramatic, frightening, exciting and sad. Hours on duty were long, off duty short, but enjoyed to the full. Older people who were wives and mothers must have found life very different and difficult to carry on. But we were young and found meeting so many new acquaintances interesting to say the least!! One particular nostalgic and sad memory remains through. 'I was dashing to catch a train after my day off and suddenly met a great friend, John England. We exchanged a few quick words and I had to go on night duty. I never saw him again as a few weeks later I was told he had been 'killed in action'".

Sheila Smith nee Woodhouse who was a pupil at Hemsby School during the war told me she was given the job of leading some reluctant younger children to school from Hemsby Common down North Road. Sheila had heard that Winterton had been machine gunned earlier and was alarmed when she heard shooting and the sound of an aeroplane. She looked up and recalls seeing a yellow German plane flying very low. There were few buildings on North Road at the time and she pushed the children into the hedge to take cover. Fortunately, her group was not shot at and she remembers seeing the pilot look back over his shoulder when he passed them. Being older than her charges the potential horror of the situation so upset Sheila that she was taken to the Manse to recover but her charges got to school without her seemingly unconcerned.

Sheila's father, Ted, was in the Home Guard and he saw a soldier fire at a German plane with a rifle. He felt this was a bad move as the Germans would return and the same November night which was foggy several bombs fell. Ted put his 'tin hat' on and went to see the damage. Fortunately some bombs had not exploded and he noted their positions. Sheila thinks there were two horses killed that night but there were no human casualties in Hemsby. Later, when the bomb disposal men came to clear the bombs, P.C. Fred Lister asked Sheila to go round all the houses in Common Road where she lived to warn of the bombs being blown up. Although the Woodhouse's lived nearest to the explosion the only damage sustained was the catch being blown off the shed door but a house further up the road had windows broken by the blast.

Cecil Hall and Ted Woodhouse in Home Guard Uniform (Photograph Sheila Smith's Collection)

Although her mother was not a net maker before the war Mrs. Woodhouse was recruited to make camouflage nets for the army. String and twine were issued to them from a net warehouse at Winterton with Sheila and Ted loading the bobbins and mother weaving the nets.

The Woodhouse family had several men billeted on them during the war. Sheila remembers "one Mexican American who was very nervous and 'frightened of his own shadow.' He did not like to eat with us and we found out why later. He didn't know how to use a knife and fork but we more or less educated him into this art."

"We had two further Americans, one of these was a Master Sergeant called Emile. He got very upset when his friend who received an injury was ordered back to the U.S.A. Emile got very drunk and emotional and had to be restrained by another soldier. The next day Emile begged us not to tell the Military Police of his indiscretion. I remember Emile's friend was very good at drawing and I wrote him several letters. I think he was later killed in action in France."

"Later we had a British Soldier of Jewish extraction. He could play the piano wonderfully. He kept in touch with us and later his family invited me to stay in London with them. My mother thought I was only 15 at the time and had not travelled much beyond Yarmouth, but I jumped at the chance. Our lodger's family had a music shop in Stoke Newington and his father and I toured London by bus. The thing I remember most was the Mayor's Ball at the Town Hall which was far more sophisticated and grand than anything I had seen in Norfolk. Although I did not attend the Ball personally I saw the beautifully dressed men and women arriving. This was shortly after the War ended."

Peter Matthews who lives in Caister but was born in Hemsby told me about his father, Arthur, who was a veteran of World War I. He was a railway signalman by day and a Sergeant in the Home Guard by night. Peter recalled his father kept detonators to blow up the railway bridge under the bed along with grenades and Sten Guns in their house on Newport Road. This thought now horrifies Peter. He told me that there was a diesel generator on the corner of Back Market Lane and Newport Road for a 'Search Light Emplacement' and a Bofors Anti Aircraft Gun. There were listening posts, reporting stations and radars most of which were operated by women members of the forces.

Peter told me that when he went with his father to the Station where Arthur discussed with Lieutenant Chinnery their exercise planned for the following Sunday to 'capture' the Radar Station at Winterton from its guards. Peter said he 'knew all about this from a boy at school who was told of it by his dad'. He continued by saying that Mr. Chinnery swore and was angry that his efforts to defend the Realm were not taken seriously enough.

Peter Matthews said his father was annoyed to have two service people billeted in his house whereas people with larger properties seemed to be excused. However, he said the two Wrens followed by two Americans were 'brilliant' and no trouble. His mother, Elsie, was a good cook and the dishes mostly containing rabbit were acceptable to her enforced tenants.

David Cook told me that much of the accommodation at the Holiday Camps and elsewhere was occupied by the military. They tended to be posted to war zones after training. The forces that were intended to defend the country were largely changed to the invasion force for D-Day. There was a practice firing range in the depression north of Hemsby Gap which was levelled in the 1970s for a car park. There was much military training going on in the Dunes north of Winterton and 'street fighting' was practiced in the bombed-out parts of Middlegate in Yarmouth.

David told me that he heard that there were heavy guns based on Hemsby Fen which fired over the beach. There were said to be an Officer and an N.C.O. on top of the church tower directing fire but he heard that a boat on the beach was damaged by these guns.

I was also told there were paths through the minefields on the sand hills. Sally Durrant an eccentric lady given to drink lived in a bungalow overlooking the beach. She had a path to her door. As did P.C. Arnold an ex-policeman from London 'who knew the lot' lived in a bungalow near the gap and kept a boat on the beach for fishing. Jim Shrimplin tells me Mr. Arnold's boat was involved in rescuing 'downed' airmen.

Hemsby Hall was used by the army but was damaged by its military occupants and had to be demolished after the war. A house on Beach Road, (The Firs) was burned down in February 1940 by the carelessness of soldiers. Michael Allen told me that Hemsby had an Auxiliary Fire Service Fire Engine ironically kept in a barn at the Firs. It was manned by Stanley Turner, Tom Nicholls and others.

Lorries intended for D-Day were lined up on Hall Road and had 'stars' painted on them to prevent allied aircraft from attacking them and numbers stenciled on by soldiers living at the Hall.

With lots of young men in the Village away from parental and communal constraints led to some sexual excess and at least one house was placed as 'out of bounds to the military'. There was some scandal but to what extent it went on I am far from certain. 'One off' incidents are often remembered but do not give a balanced picture but I was told of two young women who gained 'reputations'. One was referred to as 'Searchlight Fanny' and the other called 'Five Bob Dolly, the Dollar Princess'.

Most people I spoke to said that the soldiers were friendly and happy to talk to the young people and later when the Americans arrived, they were very free offering their sweets and chewing gum to the children. I asked if there was any incidents of child molesting and was told that no one had heard of such a thing at the time and there was none reported in this area. However, there were press reports of some soldiers prosecuted for theft and drunkenness.

Mrs Marjorie Jackson nee Bishop told me she was at Seacroft Camp the day war broke out when Army Officers in gold braid commandeered the camp but she knew nothing of holding prisoners there. Seacroft had some of its huts removed and was largely used for storage of military supplies and equipment, whereas Maddieson's Camp was used to accommodate army personnel.

I was contacted by a Mr. David Harvey who told me that he was researching into the life story of a Lieutenant Ferdinand Arthur Richards, a veteran of the British Army of the First World War. He was, however a fluent German Speaker who had worked on unspecified duties in Military Intelligence up until 1919. Mr. Harvey's information suggested that Lt. Richards was re mobilised the day before the war broke out to set up an internment camp for enemy aliens in one of the holiday camps in Hemsby. Nothing further has come to light and I suspect this is one of the many plans that were quickly abandoned during the war. Perhaps it was because Hemsby was too near the east coast and aliens were sent to the Isle of Man. Lt. Richards died in 1942 and was buried in Dublin.

A RUNAWAY TRAIN PASSED THROUGH HEMSBY

The following incident was related to me by Mr. Jack Stowers at his brother's funeral in January 2008.--

Probably in the spring or summer of 1943, Mr. Stowers who had recently been promoted to be a very young fireman (17 or 18) on the former Midland and Great Northern Joint Railway operating out of Beach Station Yarmouth. His engine was one of two pulling a train of 45 trucks of American bombs landed at Immingham for the U.S.A.A.F. bombing campaign on Nazi Occupied Europe. Although these bombs did not have fuses they were a dangerous cargo. The train travelled from the Humber to South Lynn, via Melton Constable to Yarmouth, over Breydon Viaduct to Lowestoft to be unloaded at Earsham near Bungay for the big airfields near there. This was not the most direct route but the line was available and it went through lowly populated areas. They travelled mostly at night and the cabs of the engines were blacked out by dark sheets so the firebox could not be seen by enemy aircraft. It was very hot and un-comfortable on the footplate. Mr. Stowers told me that on his first journey all was going well as far as Martham. But when they got to Ormesby the Engine Driver told him check if the train was complete. Through the darkness and steam Mr. Stowers could only see two trucks attached to his train but he saw the rest of the trucks coming up the hill unattached. These stopped and rolled back towards Hemsby settling at the lowest part of the track near Thoroughfare Lane. After re-coupling the train they found the Guard in the 'Brake Van' with the trucks was terrified as his brakes were not adequate to stop such a big train of loose coupled trucks.

Arthur Matthews reported opening the gates at Hemsby Station 'In the Middle of the Night' to let a military train through but saw only a short train without lights on the back Next he heard a 'woosh' as some un-accompanied trucks went through the station. He then heard another 'woosh' as some more trucks with guard's van with lights attached went through. This situation concerned him greatly and he phoned through to Ormesby to stop the train. Arthur wondered what might have happened to Hemsby if anything had really gone wrong with this train.

Mr. Stowers said that these trains were reduced to 30 trucks and two went along this route every night up to the end of the war. Should there be a danger of air-raids the engine driver was told to slow down to ten miles an hour so the train would not jump the rails. If the train crew were in severe danger they were to stop and shelter under the tender. They were also told not to bank the fire up in the engine so that it would emit sparks giving its position away to enemy aircraft.

The uneven curving railway track running west of Martham Road caused the train carrying bombs to become uncoupled. (Photograph M. Pickard)

Above: The Signal Box in Ormesby where Mr. Stowers would have discovered he had 'lost' most of his train. (Photograph John Bull)

This aspect of the use of the Midland and Great Northern Railway during World War II is largely unknown but there is a great deal of evidence to confirm it. Indeed in a book called "By Rail to Victory" published by the L.N.E.R. after the war, it was stated that five trains of up to sixty four trucks used the M & G.N. line on 'D-Day' alone. The journalist and broadcaster, Mr. Tony Mallion told me that his grandfather Ernest Mallion spoke of trains carrying munitions held overnight at Gorleston-on Sea Railway Station.

The road system in Britain was very limited and inadequate to the needs of the War Effort. Petrol and rubber were in short supply but coal and steel for railways could be obtained within these islands, hence the transport system relied upon trains.

Left Fred Chinnery and Arthur Matthews were Lieutenant and Sergeant of the Hemsby Home Guard; Station Master & Signalman in civilian life. (Peter Matthews Collection)

Right: Most cameras were confiscated during the war but Mr. Stowers found a picture of train crews who saw war duty taken at Beach Station in 1947. They are (top left to right Tom Chilvers, Jim Doyle, Alf Herod, Jack Stowers, (ground level) Fred Page, Harry Sheen, Ned Woodcock, Ben Sillett and Lou Attoe.

THE AIR WAR OVER HEMSBY

Mr. Bob Collis, Aviation Historian of Lowestoft, told me that Hemsby was located in the Norwich Police Division in WW II and Civil Defence recorded 17 air raids from 15/8/1940 to 4/3/45.

Some Recorded Incidents

A JU88 German Bomber crashed in the sea off Hemsby damaged by ground fire from a light anti-aircraft battery at Caister 30/7/42 being one of the last 'Baedecker Raids'. The crew of four survived; one swam ashore and three came in by dinghy all were taken prisoner.

19th March 1943.	A parachute mine damaged 50 houses in Hemsby. See above
7th May 1943	Two people killed at Winterton and a search light camp at Scratby machine gunned.
7th May 1943.	Roland Edmunds injured by machine gun fire from an aircraft.
9th Oct. 1943.	Stirling Bomber crash landed in sea of Hemsby all seven crew escaped. See next page.
29th Sept 1944.	One of the first V2 Rockets landed on the shoreline at Hemsby 2 shops, 6 houses and 50 wooden structures damaged.
4th March 1945	Hemsby was strafed by German plane but no harm recorded.

A MYSTERY CRASH LOST FROM THE RECORDS

Mr. Bob Collis and Alan Hague of Flixton Aviation Museum have seen the Civil Defence records from Norwich Police showing that a plane not described or listed, crashed on Hemsby Beach on July 28th 1943. The files reported the incident at 13.45 hours so probably crashed or had a forced landing 1-2 hours earlier. The file stated 'crew safe'. This indicating it was not a single seat aircraft. All they know it was not German or an American Heavy Bomber. Was this a plane on a secret mission?

A Westland Lysander, (short take-off and landing aircraft) which was similar to those flown from the air strip on Martham Road. They could have guns mounted in their wheel 'spats and a machine gun could be fired from the open cockpit facing backwards.

The Norfolk Historical Atlas mentions a Second World War airstrip in Hemsby (off the Martham Road) operating Lysander aircraft, probably for spotting enemy ships. These planes were also used to land arms and agents into and out of occupied Europe in secret. Flying from nearly as far to the east as it was possible to get in England was obviously a good idea but I can find no records of these operations.

Towards the end of the war German tactics were to bomb and strafe military targets with Focke-Wulf 190s which flew low and fast to avoid radar and Allied fighters. However, they proved not very precise in their targeting. Their bombs were relatively small but it was almost impossible to prevent such raids and their raids could be fatal.

'C FOR CHARLIE'S' LUCKY LANDING IN THE SEA OFF HEMSBY

The following incident was related to me by Mr. Philip Dyson and written up in the October 15th 1993 Yarmouth Mercury - On the night of the 8th- 9th October 1943 Pilot Officer Dyson and his crew of a further six men took off in a Short Stirling (C for Charlie) of 196 Squadron from R.A.F. Witchwood near Ely as part of diversionary raid to Bremen in Germany. Two of their engines failed and they limped back to England hoping to land at a suitable airfield but it was foggy, and they were losing height. All P/O Dyson could make out was the shore line so he landed the plane in the sea parallel to the breaking waves some two hundred yards off the beach. He was knocked out by the impact but as his aeroplane went under the water he revived. The plane rose above the waves for long enough and all the crew got into a rubber dingy and rowed to the shore where Mr. Alec Gillespie bravely had come through the minefield with a torch to guide them to safety not knowing if they were friend or foe at the time. Mr. Dyson told me that they were very well looked after by WRENS at the Seadell or Sea Gate building and were given the ladies dressing gowns to wear when they took off their wet flying suits. Much of the wreck remained on the beach until it was cleared in 1970.

A Short Stiring Bomber similar to the one that crash landed off Hemsby Beach

HEMSBY SCHOOL SECOND WORLD WAR.

(Photograph Mrs. P. Wacey's Collection)

Note windows taped to reduce the risk of flying glass should bombing occur.

Top Row: left to right. Alec Wilson, Bobby Watson, Unknown Evacuee nicknamed Rubber Neck, Neville Rogers, Harold Tennant, Geoffrey James, Chris Miatt.

Girls standing: Sylvia Long, Amy Porter, Nora Bessey, Doris Cook, Unknown, Jean Gislam, Sheila Woodhouse, Doris Dyble, Patricia Fakes, Peggy Myhill, Enid King.

Girls sitting: Freda (Dick) Lister, Elsie Chaney, Janet Smith, Sheila Welch, Janet Boggis, Audrey Grapes, Maureen Gibbs, Josephine ? Could be Stone evacuee staying with Jack & Florrie King.

Front Row: Peter Matthews, Frank Watson, Ronnie Wymer, Norman Green, Jack Fakes, Brian ? Evacuee, Alec Powles.

The war in Europe ended on 8th May 1945 but continued until August 15th in the Far East. Shortages remained and many men remained in the military. People continued to be killed after hostilities ended. Rationing continued until 1954 and the severe winter of 1947 caused much misery.

Sources :- "Air Raid The enemy air offensive against East Anglia 1939 -45" Michael J. F Bowyer (Patrick Stephens Limited 1992), Mr. Alan Hague of Flixton Aviation Museum, Mr. Bob Collis of Lowestoft, 'Great Yarmouth Front Line Town 1939-1945' by Charles G Box (The official Account of the A.R.P. activities and enemy action within the County Borough of Great Yarmouth), the Yarmouth Mercury and various anecdotes passed to me as stated

Andrew Fakes (November 2010) George Beech's contribution to the 'War Effort was to write the following poem in the Norfolk dialect'. I am indebted to Rosemary Thurston who found it in a deed box in Galveston Texas U.S.A in the papers of Mr. Alfred Abner who she met during the war. George printed and published 'Our Home Guard' as a single sheet and sold it for three pence. The proceeds were in aid of Norfolk War Charities. Lieutenant Fred is Mr. Fred Chinnery Station Master.

NORFOLK HOME GUARD

They ha' jined up for duration
In this funny sort o' war
Where the poor ole civvy people take the knocks,
An' they're longing for the barges
Full of Jerries come ashore,
An' meet 'em on the beach, and give 'em socks.

When they ha' done their job in workshop,
Arter work they put on khaki battle-dress,
So wi' rifles at 'the ready'
They do night guard wi'out pay,
An then wait for some aggressor to aggress.

Hear the good ole colour sergeant
Wi' his ole sweats awful bark,
Haller {hollow] "Slope! Ya may ha' bruk yer mother's hearts,
But mine ya'll never break me lads
I ken see ya in the dark.
So now, smack yer blinkin' butts an' do it smart!"

If Lord Gort could see our section
As they muster on parade,
Wi' Bryl-creemed hair a shinin' in the sun;
An' their bloomin' smart appearance,
Showin' strides they all ha' made,
He'd promote Lieutenant Fred for What he've done.

Though we hope the call to action
Will never made on you,
For to stop the paratroops in field an' loke,
By the badge you wear so proudly,
We are sure you will be true,
An will fight an' die if need be, for yer folk.

Now boys, when the war is over,
An' you all hand in your arms,
To lose uniform and gaiters will be hard;
But I bet there'll be some jokin',
When you go back to yer farms
An' tell 'em yer doin's wi' the Guard.

As an epilogue I'll mention,
That they're planning' in Whitehall,
To give all on ya a medal for yer stunt;
For the long an' dreary watches,
When you answered Duty's call
An stood guard o'er kith an' kin on our home front.

THE HUMAN COST OF WORLD WAR II IN HEMSBY

No citizen of Hemsby was killed within the parish boundaries but I believe six people died here as a direct result of the war.

The Yarmouth Mercury reported the burial of Janus Galli (26) a Latvian Seaman whose body came ashore on the Hemsby Beach from the Steamer Tautmala or Tautmila which was bombed by German Aircraft. He was buried in Hemsby Churchyard on 10/2/1940.

Mr. Kenneth Chaney told me his father, Arthur, was allowed on to the beach during the war, going through the mine field on showing his pass to the sentry. He saw an open boat being blown on to the beach by an easterly gale. It was almost capsized near the shore but landed without turning over. There was a body in the boat, blue with cold but otherwise unmarked. The man was wearing a boiler-suit as though he had been working in the engine room. The lifeboat was very well equipped with food and water and some protective clothing. Arthur reported this to the authorities including the Receiver of Wrecks. He was able to purchase the boat for £ 3. It was about 25 feet long with copper buoyancy tanks but rather too big to be used off Hemsby Beach so Arthur used the materials for further boat building and general maintenance.

The crew of three of a Bristol Blenheim Mark IV aircraft (No. 3617) of 114 Squadron from R.A.F. Oulton (near Aylsham) were killed when it crashed about 200 yards west of the Railway embankment at Bridge Farm on Martham Road at approximately 21.30 on 9th December 1940. They were on a training flight over the North Sea when they were reported as being hit by 'friendly fire' from a Naval Patrol over the North Sea. They were:-

Warrant Officer William Ross Watson No age or relatives given but he was buried in West Norwich Cemetery so possibly a local man.

Sgt. Observer Gordon Boulton, Age 21 son of Herbert and Marion Boulton of Hoyland, Yorkshire.

Air Gunner Derek Arthur Shildrick R.A.F.V.R. Age 20 son of Arthur and Dorothie Shildrick of Stanmore.

Mrs. Amy Lines nee Porter said that the fuel tank from this plane crashed through the dairy room of their house but there was no one in it at the time. Mr. Harry Allen, the butcher, went to the wreck of the plane and pulled a man out alive from it but he died later. The fuel from the plane rendered the water from the Porter's well undrinkable for some time

The German pilot of a Focke-Wulf 190 Was killed on 7/5/1943 when his plane hit an electricity pole at Newport after bombing and strafing the village. His papers indicated his name was Willi Freudenriech. age 28 but German records state his forename as Alois. He was buried at Caister 10/5/1943 but his remains were moved to the German War Cemetery at Cannock Chase in the 1960s.

The only civilian to be killed was a girl blown up by a mine on the sand hills. Jim Shrimplin told me she attended Ormesby School with him. Her name was Sheila Read and there is a memorial in St Margaret's Church to her there. David Cook told me that he was going from Newport to Hemsby Gap to collect his father's bike when he met Sheila and her brother, both known to him as he had played with them. He thinks they were possibly on the sand hills after rabbits. The story goes that the boy stood on the mine but survived but his sister was blown to pieces. David told me she had been evacuated from Yarmouth to avoid the bombing there. The family was living in Scratby at the time. She is listed on Ormesby Burial Register as entry No. 694 as Sheila Kathleen Read age 10 of Scratby. Her funeral was on 20th July 1944 and was conducted by the Rev. T.W. Bracecamp.

The war memorial in the churchyard contains eight names of young men from Hemsby who died in military service between 1939 and 1945. There are twenty names on the World War I Memorial.

Many of the details below were gathered from the Commonwealth War Graves Commission Website www.commonwealthwargravescommission.org and www.roll-of-honour.com/Norfolk/Hemsby

Armes C. S. Cubitt Stanley. Private, Driver, R.A.S.C. Age 28 died 17/11/40 in hospital as a result of leg injuries and shock following a road accident (injured by insecure load.). He was the son of the late Mrs. R Armes and was brought up by his grandmother Mrs. C. Loades of White House, Hemsby. Since his marriage he had lived with his wife at Bell Yard Martham. They had one little girl aged ten months. Up to his call-up he had worked at Bradfield's Stores, Martham. He is buried at Martham churchyard. (Yarmouth Mercury)

Cubitt Armes (Mrs. Alice
Armes Collection)

England J. K. M.B.E. John Kay. Age 22 Died 24/3/45. He was a Lieutenant in the Royal Armoured Corps Parachute Regiment. Only child of Edward Arthur & Marion McCulloch England (Mr. England was Headmaster of Hemsby School). John was buried at Riechwald Forest Cemetery Germany

(From London Gazette 27/2/1945) John England's citation reads. The King has been graciously pleased to give order for the following appointment to the Most Excellent the Membership of the British Empire in recognition of gallant and distinguished service in the field.

I quote from a newspaper (probably the Yarmouth Mercury) supplied by Mrs. H Gallaway of Blofield re the report of his death. "He was educated Yarmouth Grammar School where he was awarded the Ferrier Prize for 'Keenness', and in July 1940 joined the Kings Cross Branch of the Westminster Bank and before volunteering in August 1941 for a young soldiers tank battalion. He

John K. England C 1944. Mr R. Kinns Collection.

had passed the first part of the Banker's Institute examination. He received his commission through Sandhurst in December 1942, after service with the Border Regiment, volunteered in October 1943 for paratroop training.

JUMPED ON D-DAY EVE.

Lieut. England jumped with his battalion on the night before D Day and was ambushed and taken prisoner the next day while on solo patrol. He spent a month in a prison camp before escaping by jumping from a moving train while on the way to Germany. After a month walking by night through France he reached the American Lines.

After a period of leave Lieut. England went as intelligence officer with the 6th Airborne Division to the Ardennes when Runstedt made his drive, and among the prisoners he interrogated was a German sergeant major who took part in the rescue of Mussolini. He crossed the Rhine with his battalion and news of his death was received shortly afterwards.

Lieut. England had decided to make the Army his career and was gazetted in the Regular Army in January. He was a member of the Albert Lodge of Freemasons."

The awful irony of the situation was as Mr. England Senior said that he had a letter from the Colonel of John's Regiment to say that his son had been killed by debris falling from an Allied glider which had been severely damaged by ground fire.

Gibbs C. E. Charles Edwin. Leading Seaman Royal Naval Patrol Service H.M. Trawler 'Lord Selbourne' Age 29 died 31/3/1941. He was son of Charles & Trurza Gibbs of Hemsby Husband of Nelly Gibbs of Pill Somerset. Recorded on the Lowestoft Naval Memorial.

Gibbs G. (Gordon) He lied about his age to sign on in 1940, under the name of Gordon McPeake. He served on H.M.S. Encounter in the Battle of the Java Sea. Captured and survived in Japanese hands until his death 12/4/1945 age 22 or 23. He was buried at Ambron Island Indonesia.(The graves were believed to have been destroyed by Tsunami 2004.) He is listed as son of Gordon and Bridget Gibbs Hemsby Norfolk

Hemsby School Football Team 1932-33. A successful year for the school team and there seem to have been thirteen of them, They are:- back row left to right Albert Smith, Donald Wymer, Stanley Long, Timmy Woodrow, Middle Row Gilbert Bessey, [Killed when a bolting Horse in 1936] Donald Humphrey, John Joice, (Killed in a plane crash in Italy January 1948 with his wife. They were delivering a DeHaviland Dove to Indian Air Lines) John Wyer, Leslie Wymer, front row John Crowe, Tom Chaney, Russell King, Gordon Gibbs (who died in Japanese hands)

Ives D .J. Douglas Julius Age 21 Died 12/9/44. Flight Sergeant (Engineer) Royal Air Force Volunteer Reserve. Son of Sidney Arthur & Louisa Ives of Hemsby. Buried Milan War Cemetery.

Miatt G.W.B. Geoffrey William Buchanan. Boy First Class Royal Navy Age 17. Died 23/10/42 serving on H.M.S. Phoebe which was torpedoed with the loss of 159 lives He is buried at Pointe Noire European Cemetery Congo. His parents had moved from Middlesex in 1936 and kept the Nelson Café Hemsby Gap. Geoffrey gained a scholarship to H.M.S. Mercury at Hamble.

Geoffrey Miatt (Chris Miatt's Collection)

Smith T.P. Trevor Patrick. Died aged 20 8/6/40. He was an 'Air Fitter' on Royal Navy H.M.S. Glorious in the Norwegian Campaign. He was the son of William James and Gladys Mary Smith of Hemsby. Recorded on Lee-on Solent Memorial.

Smith D. C. Derek Clowes. Flight Sergeant (Engineer) R.A.F. died 14/3/1943 age 21 years. He was buried at St Peter & Paul Churchyard Mautby. Family details as above. Michael Allen told me their mother worked for H.R. Allen Butcher delivering meat during the War. Their father was part of Smith Brothers (Wholesale Grocers) of Blackfriars Road Great Yarmouth. Michael also said that he thought that the Smith family were related to Mrs. England the Headmaster's wife and to Harry Wharton of Church Farm, Mautby

Mr. Wharton was in charge of a group who were to be the 'British Resistance' for the Fleggs should the Nazis invaded. I have seen an underground depot where their arms and explosives were stored in Mautby. Fortunately they were not called upon to use them.

CIVILIANS KILLED IN NEARBY PARISHES

12 year old Beryl Applegate was injured as a result of an air raid on 4/9/1940 on her home, 14 Council Houses, Somerton Road Martham. She died from her injuries in Norfolk & Norwich Hospital on 6/9/1940. She was the daughter of Charles and Phoebe Margaret Applegate. She is commemorated in the County Borough of Norwich Civilian War Dead.

The Larner sisters were photographed outside Albion House, Winterton. Katherine, standing on the right was killed and Florence, standing o the left, was blinded in the air-raid on 7/5/1943.

Two women were killed in Winterton 7th May 1943 as a result of enemy bombing of their houses. One was Edna Maud Hodds known as 'Busy Hodds'; the other was my Grandmother's sister Katherine Brown nee Larner. Her sister Florence was blinded. A short time previous to this Katherine's husband Henry, a carpenter working at Neave's of Catfield, was killed on the bends by Mill Farm, Winterton, when he was struck by an ambulance when riding his bicycle. It was thought that as it was a very windy day he was on the 'wrong side of the road seeking shelter in the lee of the hedge.'

Alice Jane Colman was killed by a bullet fired from an aircraft in Little Ormesby 11/5/1943. She was 67 years old and commemorated on Blofield & Flegg R.D.C. memorials.

The two raids on the Yarmouth area of 7th and 11th May 1943 constituted the worst week of the war for casualties in Yarmouth. Ninety two people were killed and ninety one were injured. These raids were carried out by a squadron of low-flying Focke-Wulf 190 fighter bombers which arrived without warning by avoiding radar detection. Barrage balloons were placed around Yarmouth to prevent such raids and fortunately the enemy was unable to repeat such tactics in this area again.

WORLD WAR II IN VILLAGES ADJACENT TO HEMSBY

Winterton was heavily defended with barbed wire, scaffold poles, concrete blocks, pill boxes and gun emplacements. The coast of Flegg was thought to be a likely place for a 'diversionary' invasion by sea as there was deep water mooring close the beach. Great efforts were made to defend it based on a four inch gun which was manufactured in 1909. It was set in the 'cliffs' below the old lighthouse. The decaying block houses, gun emplacements and military buildings were thought to be an eyesore and many were demolished in the mid 1960s. Coastal erosion also carried evidence of these buildings away.

At Winterton, the 200 foot radar tower attracted the attention of several enemy air raids. It was part of the CHEL (Chain Home Extra Low) system intended to detect enemy E & U boats as well as low flying aircraft which did not 'show up' on earlier Radar Systems. It was also the site of an Oboe 9000 Radar intended to improve the accuracy of Allied Bombing over Europe.

The firing ranges and minefields on the dunes north of Winterton were the sites of some fatalities through 'friendly fire' and by people straying into minefields. These accidents were largely kept quiet during the war. Of the twenty six names on Winterton War Memorial, I believe include a proportion of those who were accidently killed within the parish. However, Mr. Mervin Goffin who attended Winterton School during the war, said that, when the children in school heard an explosion they would say 'There goes another exploding dog'. Canine trespass in to the mine field was common at that time.

WINTERTON HOME GUARD c 1943

Top Row.
1 Sidney Wacey (W). 2, Claude Simmons (S) 3, Tom Knights (S) 4. George Green (S) 5. George Rump (S) .6 (R A) .Soldier. 7 (RA) Soldier . 8 Charles (Rax) Watson (W) 8 Percy Goodrum (S) 9 Dennis Gallant (S) 10 (RA) Soldier

Second From Top
1.Claude Hodds (W) 2. Walter (Punch) George (W) 3. Wilfred (Pompey) Green.(W) 4. Kenneth Haylett (W) .5 Norman Green (W) 6 Wesley Cator (S) 7. Arthur Leath (S) .8 Joe Thain (S) 9 Edward Bush (W) 10 Harry Kettle (S) 11 Harry Neave (W) 12 Harry Moll (W)

Third From Top
1.Eric Drury (S). 2 George (Toots) King (W) 3 George (Waxey) King (W) 4 (RA)(Soldier 5 Lt A England (H) 6. Capt, Silvester (RA) Comm Officer 2nd Lt Meare (S) 8. (RA) Soldier . 9 Lou Baxter (S). 10.George Dix (W) 11 George Howes (S)

Bottom Row
1 Jimmy Chapman (W) 2 Rolly Moore (S) 3 James (Dibby) Goffin (W). 4 Jimmy King (W) 5 Willie (Dutch) Green (W). 6 Ernest Slipper (S) 7. Jimmy Shreeve (S) 8 Bob Sadler (S) 9 (RA) Soldier. 10 Alec Bell (S)

Key to abbreviations (W) Winterton, (S) Somerton, (H) Hemsby .(R.A) Royal Artillery Coastal Battery

Although this picture is described as the Winterton Home Guard it may be more accurate to say it was also the Winterton Gun Crew as the men come from several other villages and some were Royal Artillerymen. Mr. Arthur England, Headmaster of Hemsby School is recorded as a Lieutenant but was later promoted to Major. They manned the 4 inch gun set in the hills below Winterton Lighthouse. (Mr. John Green's collection)

Left. A Pill Box covering the road from the beach to Winterton. (John Green's Collection). Right. The former block-house at Somerton which controlled the fires and lights on the 'Q Site' there. (A. J. Fakes 2010)

The Admiralty set up a 'Starfish' Decoy Site on Winterton and Somerton Holmes. This was made by Sound City Films of Shepperton. It consisted of a series of lights and burning troughs of oil and coal so that it would appear to be the Port of Yarmouth at night to enemy aircraft. This effect was also helped by the fact that Horsey Mere looked like Breydon Water to bomber pilots. The dunes and marshes were bombed by the Luftwaffe as many as seven times resulting in no injury to any one or damage to the war effort.

Geoff Smith and his family were living at Mill Farm, Winterton, during the War. His home was remote from that village by the bends on the Hemsby road. It was felt to be safer than in the villages and many people gravitated there during bombing raids. They had people who had been bombed out stay with them and his family had over a dozen people sleeping in the house on several occasions. Although Geoff witnessed a 'stick' of bombs fall near the lighthouse without concern, he was considerably traumatized as a child when he was shot at by a German plane. His sister saved him by pushing him through a hedge. He told me that, after the war that he and his school friends had great pleasure in collecting spent bullets. They would take the remaining powder out. This was taken to school and put in milk straws and thrown on to the open fire with spectacular results.

Not all German airmen were keen to prosecute the war. Douglas Brown in his book 'East Anglia 1941' recounts that " 'the crew of four of a Junkers JU88 which crashed at Somerton in late January 1941 told their captors 'We are in good old England at last. We feel at home now.'"

Mr. Percy Trett of Great Yarmouth told me that he was living at Loveday's Estate at Scratby when he was at school rather than his normal address in Yarmouth. On his birthday 11th May 1943 he had stayed behind to open his birthday presents. He normally travelled to Yarmouth with a Mrs. Blythe who kept a delicatessen shop in Central Arcade. Mrs. Blythe was killed in an air raid on her way to work.

There was a Radar Station immediately in front of Mrs. Chipperfield's Post Office on the Cliffs at Scratby. It consisted of several Nissen Huts surrounded by a thick brick blast wall with the radar reflectors poking over the top. There were several other Nissen Huts about three hundred yards further inland also surrounded by blast walls, I am told the information gathered was analysed, mostly by female military personnel. I remember a heavy machine gun on a fixed base in a field behind the huts. I understand this was an Orlekin Gun and there were several others throughout the district. I recall a gun emplacement on the cliffs on what some people still refer to as Gun Hill in Scratby. David Cook thinks this was a gun originating from World War I.

The open highlands on Rollesby Heath had thick wooden poles fixed across posts about three feet high wired together to prevent gliders and aeroplanes from landing.

Mr. Jim Shrimplin of Ormesby told me there were two Bofors Anti-Aircraft Guns on the east side of the road between Hemsby and Ormesby at the top of the hill. He

The high brick blast wall surrounding the Radar Station in front of Mrs. Chipperfield's Post Office on the Cliffs at Scratby. (Francis Frith Postcard)

remembers a corrugated iron cook house and a bell tent for the gun crews. There was a Lewis Gun emplacement in the hedge on the east side of the road. There were also acoustic detectors in the field behind where the Meteorological Station site stood also there were three Radio Direction Finding Towers. These were wooden structures on brick bases and they were about 25 feet high. Two of these were operated by R.A.F. crews the personnel being billeted with families in Hemsby & Ormesby The third tower was operated by U.S, forces and was used only briefly.

Jim remembers a Bristol Blenheim aircraft crashed on the beach at California and a Fairey Fulmer crash landing at 'Frog's Hall' north of Thoroughfare Lane. He believes the S.O.E. 'covert' flying into Europe took off from Starch Grass Meadow, Heigham Holmes the 'other' side of Martham ferry.

On Ormesby Green a brick pill box was built opposite the King's Head and a large oval trench was dug as a defence measure. A further pill box was built at the junction of North Road and Station Road and a Fougasse was located in the bank adjacent to it. This consisted of several 5 gallon drums of petrol with explosives attached. The theory was that it should be detonated if an enemy tank passed. There was also a searchlight situated in Nova Scotia road.

A Miles Magister training aircraft landed in the field beside the Methodist Chapel in Scratby. It had been taken by German Prisoners of War who had escaped from Shap Fell. They stole the plane in Lincolnshire but ran out of petrol. They were walking into Ormesby to get some more fuel. They had covered their buttons with silver paper to make themselves look official! They claimed to be Dutch but when it was realized that their plane had been stolen, they were arrested.

King George VI and Lord Gort (Chief of Staff) came to Ormesby to inspect the Newfoundland Artillery which was based at Ormesby Lodge and Ormesby Hall. Jim remembers the VIPs. were in an open car proceeded by two 5.5 inch anti aircraft guns. Jake Clark of the Newfoundland men remained in Britain to become post master at Fleggburgh.

Jim recalls an extensive anti-aircraft site being set up at Mautby to counter the V1.Flying Bomb threat. There were numerous wooden buildings on this site and Mrs. Shirley Travis of Filby told me that civilians 'squatted' in these huts after the war because of the extreme shortage of houses. The Yarmouth Mercury stated in the November 23rd 1946 edition that the residents of these properties were originally denied a coal ration but a petition to the Queen in 1947 resulted in Herbert Morrison overturning this decision.

The consequences of World War II tragically continued for many years not only in those who were injured in body and mind by the fighting. I have found a record of two Winterton men dying after V.E. Day (May 8th 1945). George Baker and Henry Popay died on 8th July 1945.on the Royal Naval Trawler 'La Nataise' This was a French boat which its crew brought over to Britain in 1940 and was commandeered by the Royal Navy. Ronnie Haylett advised me that they were taking the boat to Scotland for decommissioning and were 'run down' by a Warship but the Commonwealth War Graves states that this accident happened in the English Channel and the ship was the S. S. Helencrest but I cannot find any details of this vessel.

In July 28th 1945 'Yarmouth Mercury' an inquest is reported on Private Peter Thomas Lawrence of Feltwell, Norfolk, who died on an exercise on the Winterton Firing Range on the Monday of that week. The Norfolk County Coroner, Mr. G. W. Barnard recorded a verdict that "death was due to multiple injuries caused by the explosion of a land mine in an unmarked minefield which he entered in the course of his duties while engaged in a field firing exercise, not knowing the area was mined." The Coroner observed, as part of his verdict that this was the second death in the same area, and suggested the military authorities should see that the wire was repaired around the minefield by those damaging it. Private Lawrence had entered through a broken section. The Coroner felt that an officer should point out the minefield when allocating the range for exercise. (Y,M.)

The June 8th 1946 The Yarmouth Mercury also reported on the Inquest on the death of of Sapper Arthur William Horham of Wood Green North (London). He was clearing mines at Winterton with a metal detector and the Coroner was satisfied that the correct procedure was being followed but accidents happen possibly through human error. (Y.M.)

The Yarmouth Mercury recorded on August 3rd 1946 that three Sappers were killed by a mine at Horsey. They were Corporal Arthur Sidney White (28) of Cowes, Isle of Wight, Sapper Walter Kenneth Gilbert (19) of Swansea and Sapper Sidney Sullivan (19) of Pontypool.

January 1947 a German P.O.W., Willi Nelseen was killed at Horsey when clearing the beach there of mines. (Y.M.)

I have also seen records of people blown up by mines at Yarmouth and Caister

Brian Hewitt told me of some boys at were having a bonfire at Winterton and various things were thrown on the bonfire. There as an explosion when something flew out and hit Owen Jenkins, the policeman's son. He was lucky enough to escape with only a broken arm.

And as late as the Easter of 1952 Walter Denis (Punch) George, a coal merchant and lorry driver of Winterton was killed on the Dunes when he struck a mine while he was digging for scrap metal. He was particularly looking for brass bullets.

Punch George and his lorry as well as being a carrier he transported fisherman to Yarmouth, workers to various sites, people to the speedway and to Hemsby Institute to see film shows. (M .Woodhouse Collection)

Andrew Fakes
(November 2010)

HEMSBY TRADGEDIES

There have been many disasters and sudden deaths in Hemsby but, where they have not been forgotten they have not been recorded chronologically. I am attempting to remedy this situation but it will involve going through many editions of the local press. Herewith an incomplete list

1842 Nine men lost at Newport after the overturning of a Beachman's boat off Newport. (D. Higgins)

The May Gale of 1860 being unexpected at that time of the year caused many drowning along the East Coast.

World War I. About 200 young men of the Village enlisted. 20 are recorded as having died

March 1922 11 year old Leonard James Knights killed on Railway Bridge. (Y.M) His funeral No.479 was recorded in Hemsby Church registry 28/3/1922.

5/8/29 Mr A. W. Francis of Martham was suffocated following a sand fall at Hemsby

June 1936 14 Year old Gilbert Noel Bessey was killed when a horse bolted at Home Farm. (Y.M.)

1939-45.Six people died in Hemsby as result of accidents and hostilities during World War II. A Latvian sailor's body was washed up on the beach, Feb 1940. Three R.A.F. men, one German pilot died as a result of air crashes and a 10 year old civilian girl died after being blown up by a mine. See section on World War II

April 1946 David Glanville Turner aged 3 died as a result of an accident involving a Military Dispatch Rider. (Y.M)

August 1947 Eight year old David Malcolm Dean of Islington drowned after being swept out to sea on car inner tube despite several attempts to save him .(Y.M)

January 1948 Benjamin Arthur Moll, a retired deep sea fisherman aged 73 of Hemsby and described at his inquest 'deaf mute' was killed on the railway line at Martham. The driver of the train said he braked and whistled but as Mr Moll's back was to the train they collided. He was believed to be looking for pieces of coal for his fire. (Y.M.)

1949 George Thurtle Junior was killed by a collapsing chimney stack when Hemsby Hall was being demolished. He is recorded in the burial of St. Margaret's Church Ormesby as No.778, George Robert Thurtle of Westholm, Ormesby St Margaret Funeral 2/8/49 Age 46 (killed in Hemsby)

January 1950. Alice Lillian Williams found dead as a result of malnutrition even though there was plenty of food in the house. Mrs Williams and her husband Basil were recluses and were no registered with any doctor and had not left the house for about six months. (Y.M.)

1971 Doctor Peter Drinkwater was accused of the murder of his mistress Carole Califano off Winterton Road Hemsby where she died of a combination of alcohol and drugs. Dr. Drinkwater was found not guilty of murder but guilty of manslaughter and was sentenced to 12 years imprisonment at St Albans Crown Court. The Judge saying that, as a doctor, his behaviour was totally irresponsible. (E.D.P.)

January 1978 Ronald and Irene Brown died in a bungalow fire at Newport. Mr Brown is believed to have returned from working at Cantley Sugar Factory when he made up the fire but he sat down and went to sleep. The coals fell onto the carpet which gave off toxic fumes and the house was severely damaged. (A.J.F)

July 1995. A triple murder occurred on Barleycroft. There is much information about this but I feel it is too recent and too 'raw' a subject to be recounted here.

Any further information appreciated.

Andrew Fakes,   72, Lawn Avenue, Gt. Yarmouth NR30 1QW

OTHER NOTABLE CITIZENS OF HEMSBY

Many interesting characters lived in Hemsby over the years. I list some of them below.

Mr. Gilbert Daniel Green (pictured in 1976) sometimes known as Martin. He ran a large and successful shop on North Road, Hemsby for many years. Gilbert was elected as Chairman of the Parish Council for a couple of years in spite of the fact he spoke in a nasal and staccato voice and was not always understood

Left. A meeting of Hemsby Parish Council circa 1978. Left to Right. George Jermany, Judy Adkins, who typed out George Beech's original manuscript of his book, Lily Guest, Parish Clerk and Brian Ernest King Chairman of the Council. (Photograph A.J. Fakes.)

Right. (Leofric) Ralph Hunt, Gardener and Parish Councilor. He was a well meaning, if naïve man but his deafness led him into misunderstandings and mockery. He is reputed to have said at a Parish Council Meeting that Hemsby should not provide litter bins as it would encourage people to bring their rubbish here! (Truly lateral thinking)

The man with white tee shirt and life jacket was P.C. Herbert (Pete) Parsley. Although not a swimmer or a boatman he was largely responsible for bringing a lifeboat to Hemsby as the first chairman of Hemsby Inshore Rescue Service in 1976.

On the right is Hemsby's first lifeboat which was a modest affair. There is now a full size inshore and a secondary life boat with boat house at Hemsby Gap. (Photographs A.J. Fakes 1976)

Left: Arthur Fakes Shopkeeper and Beachcomber. One of a number of people who spend much of the life on the beach collecting whatever the North Sea threw up be it fish, timber or semi precious stones. Over about seventy years he collected several pounds of amber (pictured).

Much timber was collected for building or as fire wood. Arthur reckoned that he got warm three times from beach timber; Firstly, by carrying it off the beach, secondly, sawing it up and thirdly from burning it on the fire. His wife, Daisy, raised funds for 'Guide Dogs for the Blind' by giving the fees she got from her talk 'The Trials of a Beach Comber's Wife' which went down well in Women's Institutes etc.

Mr. Bob Turner of Newport collected almost every piece of wood he could find and storing it in his yard, gaining the nickname 'Jewson'. He said he collected it because it was 'a hazard to navigation'.

In later years containerization of cargo and few ship wrecks resulted in less valuable flotsam and jetsam.

Coins could also be found on the beach, originally by the wind blowing sand away from lost money but in recent years metal detecting has become popular.

Mrs. Ada Elizabeth Fakes unveiling a seat (made by George Beech) outside the Doctor's Surgery in 1962 in memory of her late husband Arthur. She went on to live to be 106 years old and gained brief international fame when she took a ride in a helicopter the day before her 105th birthday in 1986. This made the 'And finally' item of news broadcasts in Australia, Canada, New Zealand and the U.S.A. Next to her is Miss Ada King who went to Hemsby School and became a pupil teacher. She became headmistress of Rollesby School, a post she held for many years. She was chairman of the Parish Council and of the Women's Institute. I am told she could keep order wonderfully without raising her voice at all. The man on the far right is Doctor Patrick (Paddy) Rotchford. He was born in Ireland he was for many years the General Practitioner for Hemsby and spent his retirement in the village.

Henry (Harry) Day opening caravan door   He was a printer from East London. He set up a Youth Club and Summer Camp in caravans off St. Mary's Road, under the name of 'The Young Citizen's Guild. He maintained a disciplined group of children who performed many useful tasks in Hemsby such a litter clearance, first aid, looking after lost children and helping at Village functions. Harry loved to be 'at the centre of things' in his own uniform. He would rush about in his Land Rover assisting the Police and 'Rescue Services'. He was seldom seen without a cigarette in his hand. He did a great deal of good and was awarded the British Empire Medal in 1984 and the M.B.E in 2004 for his efforts. He seemed to be on good terms with senior policemen, politicians, magistrates and even royalty.

Mrs. Kathleen Sigee. She moved to Hemsby from Leicester and became very much involved in village life.

However, by 2009 various complaints came to light and Mr. Day was sentenced to thirteen years imprisonment on 21 counts of sexual abuse.

Left: Mr. Walter (Twoshy) Brown. He was a competent and experienced fisherman and boatman. He originally came from Sheringham shortly after the war. I'm told that he brought his furniture here in his boat and lived in a wooden bungalow overlooking the beach. He fished off Hemsby for many years without serious mishap. He taught many young men seamanship and fishing technique if they would 'crew' for him. He was supposedly called 'Twoshy' because there were two boats. The first was called 'Why Not' and Walter wanted to call his 'Too Shy' but misspelled the word 'too' as 'two'. Walter was described as 'A good old boy but he suffered from a terrible thirst!' (Picture Ted Fryatt)

Right Mr. Alec Ramer Green and dog; Farm Worker, Pig's Midwife and 'Man about Hemsby'. Alec had an ''eventful war ''as a gunner on tankers carrying high octane aviation fuel across the Atlantic for the aero planes in the Battle of Britain.

Dorothy and Frank Duffield, pictured with dog on a Norton Motor Cycle on Common Road. Frank died as a result of being electrocuted while operating a petrol pump in 1958 leaving Dorothy with five children. In spite of this she spent much of her time heavily involved in Village life, the Church, good works and fund raising for various organizations in Hemsby. She was a recipient of Royal Maundy Money from the Queen in Norwich Cathedral. She died in 2003

HEMSBY

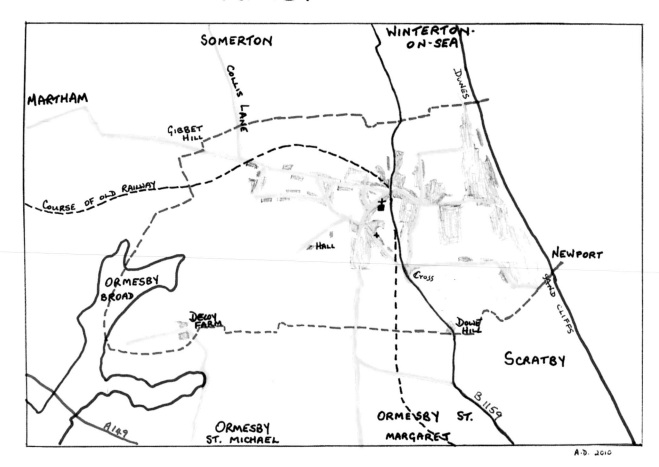

Map of Hemsby circa 1970 showing parish boundaries, the old railway line and roads (Drawn by Ann Dunning)
(Nothing definite is known about a gibbet on the Martham Road and is possibly a myth handed down)

Beach at Hemsby Gap 1960
Pictures by T.R. Fakes

A post card circa 1960 shows the pools or 'lows' which formed on the beach. They could be of sufficient size and depth for a rowing boat to navigate. They made a pleasant, warm and safe area for children to play in the water but if they were not replenished with 'fresh' sea water from time to time, they became stagnant and smelly.

From about 1980 the sand banks in the North Sea off Hemsby moved forcing a 'rip' tide which made the shore line much steeper and the sand hills, which had previously been building up, began to erode. All the bungalows on the beach or at the top of the dunes were undermined. Even the concrete anti tank blocks and "pill boxes" built early in the Second World War and buried by sand for many years were undermined by the North Sea and the ramp to the Lifeboat Shed was broken.

Mr. Walter 'Twoshy' Brown, the well known boat owner and fisherman, told me that it is almost impossible to fight the sea. As he put it "If Davy Jones wants it, he'll ****** well take it and there in't nothing you can do about it boy!"

Pictures by A. J. Fakes)

Above: George Beech's Print Shop circa 1960 built of clay lump, board and Norfolk pan tile with proverbial brick privy. (Picture by M. Pickard)

Above: Intricate wood carving by George Beech (A.J. Fakes)

Examples of George Beech's printing showing some of the commercial and social life of Hemsby.

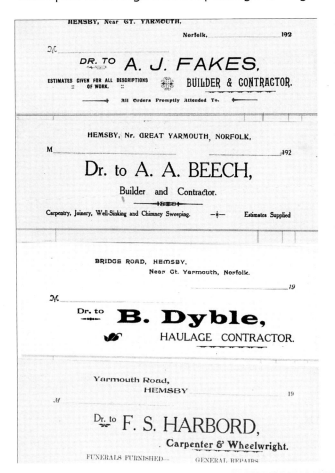

HEMSBY, Near GT. YARMOUTH,
Norfolk,_____192

M_____

DR. TO **A. J. FAKES,**
ESTIMATES GIVEN FOR ALL DESCRIPTIONS
:: OF WORK. ::
BUILDER & CONTRACTOR.

→ All Orders Promptly Attended To. ←

HEMSBY, Nr. GREAT YARMOUTH, NORFOLK,
M_____192

Dr. to **A. A. BEECH,**
Builder and Contractor.

Carpentry, Joinery, Well-Sinking and Chimney Sweeping. — Estimates Supplied

BRIDGE ROAD, HEMSBY,
Near Gt. Yarmouth, Norfolk.
_____19
M

Dr. to **B. Dyble,**
HAULAGE CONTRACTOR.

Yarmouth Road,
HEMSBY 19
M

Dr. to **F. S. HARBORD,**
Carpenter & Wheelwright.

FUNERALS FURNISHED — GENERAL REPAIRS

"PEACE IN OUR TIME."
Support The League of Nations !

You are invited to attend the
FIRST ANNUAL MEETING
of the
HEMSBY BRANCH
of—
THE LEAGUE OF NATIONS UNION
to be held in
THE BARN ROOM
ON—
THURSDAY, NOVEMBER 20th 1924
The Chair will be taken at 7. 30 p.m.

There will be an open discussion
on the work of the League : :

THE FLEGG PRESS, HEMSBY.

TRIMLEY VANGUARD
(No. 6274)
FOALED 1931

The Property of E. G. KING, Horsey.

sire HORSTEAD VANGUARD (4784)
by MORSTON GOLD GUARD (4234)
dam TRIMLEY PRINCESS PAT (12551)
by MORSTON CONNAUGHT (4590)
Record to 8th. dam.

All Mares tried at owner's risk. Fee £2 per
Mare to be paid 2nd. week in June 1936.

Groom's Fee 3/-

MINISTRY OF AGRICULTURE LICENSE 1936.

ST. MARTIN'S MISSION CHURCH
HEMSBY BEACH.

Vicar : Rev. W. H. W. Pipe. Lay Reader : Mr. E. S. Chapman.

TO OUR VISITORS.

Our Church was built mainly for the convenience of those who are spending their holidays with us on the Beach.

We have now made our arrangements for the Summer Months, and we venture to publish the particulars of our Services in the hope that you may be able to avail yourselves of some of them.

HOLY COMMUNION : Every Sunday, Wednesday and Friday at 8 a.m.
SUNG EUCHARIST : Every Sunday at 11 a.m.
EVENSONG : Every Sunday at 6.30 p.m.

It may be necessary to make some slight alterations and additions, consequent on the occasions of Saints' Days, etc., but particulars of these will be found on the Church Notice Board.

The Church is open throughout each day for Private Prayer.

The Flegg Press, Hemsby.

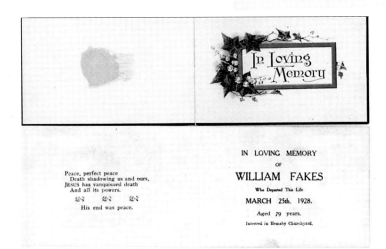

In Loving Memory

Peace, perfect peace
Death shadowing us and ours,
JESUS has vanquished death
And all its powers.

His end was peace.

IN LOVING MEMORY
OF
WILLIAM FAKES
Who Departed This Life
MARCH 25th. 1928.
Aged 79 years.
Interred in Hemsby Churchyard.

☞ KEEP THIS PROGRAMME   No............

The
Hemsby Concert Party

present

THE VARIETY SHOW

"SMILING AGAIN"

Produced by

VINCENT ARMES

(by arrangement with Abel Hayward).

Accompanist	Vera Powles
Chorus Girls	Alice Armes, Ann Dyble, Audrey Grapes, Janet Crowe, Sheila Woodhouse, Grace Turner.
Curtains	Bob Powles, Arthur Turner.

Price ... 4d.

Part One

1.	Opening Chorus		THE PARTY
2.	Dance	'Fella with an Umbrella' SHEILA DYBLE SHIRLEY ALLEN	
3.	Song	'The Tramp'	MICHAEL POWLES
4.	Play	'Bill the Burglar' BILL BRUGGER CHARLES POWLES TREVOR ARMES STUART POWLES NANCY CHANEY	
5.	Song		DEREK SMITH
6.	Scene	'The Encampment' SHEILA DYBLE SHIRLEY ALLEN with CHORUS GIRLS	
7.	Play	'Lodgings for Single Ladies' JANET CROWE MICHAEL POWLES	
8.	Song		TREVOR ARMES
9.	Song	'Just a Has-been' SHEILA WOODHOUSE	
10.	Play	'This School Question' ALICE ARMES ROSE WOODHOUSE	
11.	Dance		SALLY COLE
12.	Scene	'Gay Nineties'	CHORUS GIRLS

INTERVAL.

Part Two

1.	Song	'Game Cock'	BOB POWLES
2.	Song	ALICE ARMES SHEILA WOODHOUSE	
3.	Song	'Couple of Swells' AUDREY GRAPES DEREK SMITH	
4.	Song	TREVOR ARMES STUART POWLES CHARLES POWLES	
5.	Play	'Uncle Joseph' ANN DYBLE SHEILA WOODHOUSE VERA POWLES DEREK SMITH MICHAEL POWLES JOHN CLAYTON	
6.	Song		AUDREY GRAPES
7.	Song	'Turned Up'	THE PARTY
8.	Dance		SALLY COLE
9.	Song	'Keys of Heaven' AUDREY GRAPES SHEILA WOODHOUSE	
10.	The Yodeller		SIDNEY GREEN
11.	Play	'Lost Property' ELSIE MATTHEWS NORMAN THURTLE	
12.	Scene	'On Parade' DEREK SMITH with CHORUS GIRLS	

FINALE

GOD SAVE THE KING.

The Flegg Press, Hemsby.

Mrs A. Fakes
To G. N. Beech

1962
  To
  Preparing Oak Memorial
  Seat 6-0 × 16"
  3" moulded legs. splatted back
  with carved centre panel:
  bracketted; with iron stay.
  1×2 oak seat rails.
  2×3 Head rail. centre moulded.
  Fixed with waterproof glue.
  treated for outdoor use.

         80 hrs   5/-   20 0 0
  Timber   3 10 0
  Glue: Galv. Screws:
  Stay iron. labour in fitting 1 10 0
                              _____
                               25 - 0 - 0
  Reduction a/c   10 0 0
                              _____
                               15 - 0 - 0
  Received with thanks
  G. D. Beech   September 26/62

Left. Shows a hand written invoice and receipt for the making of a wooden seat by George Beech to Mrs. Ada Fakes as a memorial to her late husband Arthur Johnson Fakes. It took George 80 hours to make it and it stood outside the Doctor's Surgery in The Street for many hears. Right a summary of the activities of the Hemsby Hospital Supply Depot during the Great War as printed by George Beech.

HEMSBY HOSPITAL SUPPLY DEPOT.
(NORFOLK.)

THIS DEPOT was started on June 11th 1915, for the supply of Hospital requisites for wounded Soldiers & Sailors,- these included Bandages & Dressings of every description, also handkerchiefs, towels, finger-stalls, slippers, knitted swabs, socks, scarves &c.,

Consignments were sent once a fortnight to the Lady-Mayoress' WAR HOSPITAL SUPPLY DEPOT, IPSWICH, and some were given for the use of the Military stationed in Hemsby.

Although Hemsby is quite a small village of 700 inhabitants,- with the help of workers from surrounding parishes the Depot was able to supply an average consignment of 1000 articles every fortnight;

The total amount sent out during the time it was opened, (June 11th 1915 to February 28th 1919,) was 115,405.

The DEPOT was started by Miss Elsie Scrimgeour of Hemsby Hall in an unfurnished house on Dow Hill; there it was carried on twice a week till January 1916, when Hemsby Lodge was kindly offered by Mrs. Lofthouse:- this house being more centrally situated the offer was gratefully accepted.

Work went on here 3 days a week, till the house was required by the Military, when Mr. & Mrs. Walter Scrimgeour kindly placed 2 large rooms in Hemsby Hall at the disposal of the workers.

The officials of the DEPOT were:-

PRESIDENT- Mrs Walter Scrimgeour. HON. SEC. & TREASURER- Miss Elsie Scrimgeour. later Miss Southwell became HON. TREAS. until Jan. 1917, when Mrs. Bagnall-Oakeley was appointed HON. SEC. & TREAS.- Miss E. Scrimgeour and Miss Southwell having left Hemsby. The COMM-ITTEE were- Mrs. Thurgar,(CHAIRMAN) Miss Daniel & Mrs. Gilliat.- on Mrs. Gilliat leaving the county, Mrs. G. W. Daniels was elected in her place. The following workers, most of whom joined the DEPOT at the start and continued their work till it was closed, were- Lady Vincent, Miss Edis, Mrs. Thurgar, The Misses Daniel, Mrs. G. W. Daniels, Mrs. W. W. Gossage, Mrs. Hacker, Miss Shrimpling, Miss Symonds, Mrs. Jalland, Miss Parry, Mrs. Tonbridge, Miss Pardoe, Mrs. & Miss Gilliat, Miss E. Scrimgeour, & Mrs. Bagnall-Oakeley.

Funds were raised by monthly subscriptions, donations & entertainments and the total amount raised from Jan. 1916 to Feb. 1919 was £538-19-9. From June 1915 to Jan. 1916 the expenses were privately defrayed.